**W9-BID-835**

FLORIDA

FLORIDA BY ROAD

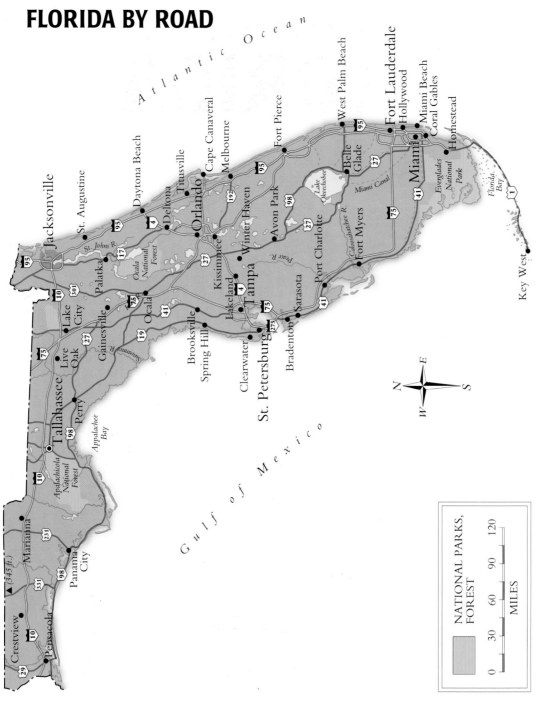

CELEBRATE THE STATES
FLORIDA

Perry Chang

BENCHMARK BOOKS

MARSHALL CAVENDISH
NEW YORK

Benchmark Books
Marshall Cavendish Corporation
99 White Plains Road
Tarrytown, New York 10591-9001

Library of Congress Cataloging-in-Publication Data
Chang, Perry.
Florida / Perry Chang.
p.   cm. — (Celebrate the states)
Includes bibliographical references and index.
Summary: Discusses the geographic features and environmental concerns, history,
government, people, and attractions of the state known as the "Sunshine State."
ISBN 0-7614-0420-1 (lib. bdg.)
1. Florida—Juvenile literature. [1. Florida.] I. Title. II. Series.
F311.3.C47   1998   975.9—dc21   97-23777   CIP   AC

Maps and graphics supplied by Oxford Cartographers, Oxford, England

Photo Research by Matthew J. & Ellen Barrett Dudley

Cover Photo: Tom Stack and Associates/John Shaw

The photographs in this book are used by permission and through the courtesy of: *Photo Researchers, Inc.*:
Andy Levin, 6-7; Jim Steinberg, 15; J.H. Robinson, 18(top); Stephen J. Krasemann, 18(bottom); M.B. Duda,
23; Jeff Greenberg, 28, 100-101, 106; Douglas Faulkner, 30; Bachman, 52-53, 89, 108; Jan Halaska, 115;
Mark C. Burnett, 119(top); H.A.Thornhill/ NAS, 119(bottom); Eunice Harris, 135; *Silver Image*: 92; Mark
Barrett, 10-11; Mark Mirko, 22; J.B. McCourtney, 59; Will Dickey/Florida Times Union, 63; Palm Beach Post,
67, 99(top); Phil Sears, 68; Steve Morton, 73, 127; C.J. Walker, 76; Andrew Itkoff, 77; John J. Lopinot, 80,
113; Bruce Fine, 84(right); Murray H. Sill, 87, 116; Jim Hargan, 103, 104. *Tom Stack and Associates*: Larry
Lipsky, 17, 20; Tess Young, 65; Brian Parker, 86(top), 123; David Young, 122. *The Image Bank*: Keith Philpott,
back cover; Tillmann, 58; Derek Berwin, 61; Frank Whitney, 70-71; Faustino, 84(left); Dann Coffey, 107; Luis
Castaneda, 110; Burton McNeely, 126. *University of Florida, From a Private Collection, Courtesy of the Harn
Museum of Art/ Landscape with Heron, oil on canvas 26x34 inches, Herman Herzog, American 1832-1932*: 32- 33.
The Granger Collection, New York: 35. *Archive Photos*: 38. *Florida State Archives*: 40, 44, 46, 47, 91, 95,
130(right). *National Portrait Gallery, Smithsonian Institute/Art Resource NY*: 42(left). *National Museum of Art,
Washington D.C./Art Resource NY*: 42(right). *Corbis- Bettmann*: 50, 64, 134. *UPI/Corbis-Bettmann*: 94, 97, 129,
130(left), 131. *Reuters/Corbis Bettmann*: 133. *Gamma Liaison*: Mike Schwarz, 99(bottom).

Printed in Italy

1   3   5   6   4   2

CONTENTS

FLORIDA IS . . . .

Florida is a beautiful place to live.

"It's got the good climate you need for all the water sports plus tennis, swimming, running. There's just a few cold months. . . . It's kind of relaxing on the shore. It's pretty laid back, listening to the water, watching the sunset."

—government official Andrew Maurey

It was once a wild, lush frontier. . .

"Vast portions of the peninsula lay remote, forbidding, inaccessible, and unsettled."   —historians Raymond Mohl and Gary Mormino

. . . but in recent times people have exploited and abused it.

"Man has butchered Florida. Every square inch of Florida is going to be covered with concrete, the way they're going."

—diving instructor Kevin Sweeney

Many different kinds of people have settled in Florida . . .

"For a lot of people in different times in their life, Florida represents a new start."   —minister Larry Reimer

"There's a kind of cosmopolitan mix, at least in larger cities, that I like—a real mix of people, with a little bit of Southern gentility mixed in, that makes it a kinder, gentler place to live."

—minister Clarke Campbell-Evans

. . . but with this diversity comes great challenges.

"Some have called Florida a holding company of independent communities in search of an identity. Building a sense of community is one of our biggest challenges."

—children's advocate Jack Levine

Florida is different things to different people. To some people, Florida is paradise. It is warm water, sun-drenched beaches, mysterious swamps, and stunning reefs. To others, it is the rural South. It is small towns, pickup trucks, and tomato fields. To still others, it is an overcrowded vacationland. It is high-rise hotels, tacky tourist traps, and bumper-to-bumper traffic.

Florida is all of these things, and much more. Jutting out several hundred miles from the continental United States toward the Caribbean, Florida is a link between North America and Latin America. It is a cultural crossroads where people of different backgrounds have mingled, traded, and sometimes fought. This is Florida's story.

1 DANGEROUS AND ENDANGERED

More than two hundred million years ago, the earth shook and created a ridge under what is now the Gulf of Mexico. During the Ice Age, much of the earth's water froze into glaciers. This lowered sea levels across the globe and eventually exposed that ridge as land. Today, the polar ice caps retain just enough of the earth's water to keep the ocean from engulfing that narrow swath of land that we call Florida.

WOODS AND WETLANDS

Florida is easily divided into two sections: the panhandle and the peninsula. Northwestern Florida, the narrow part of the state that hugs the Gulf coast south of Alabama and Georgia, is called the panhandle. The peninsula, a strip of land surrounded by water, juts out about four hundred miles into the water, separating the Gulf of Mexico from the Atlantic Ocean.

A chain of islands called the Florida Keys arcs out into the gulf from the southern tip of the peninsula. The southernmost of these islands, Key West, lies just ninety miles from the island nation of Cuba.

Florida has three natural regions: hardwood forests, pine barrens, and wetlands. Hardwood forests cover north Florida and sections of central Florida, the parts of the state with the highest

LAND AND WATER

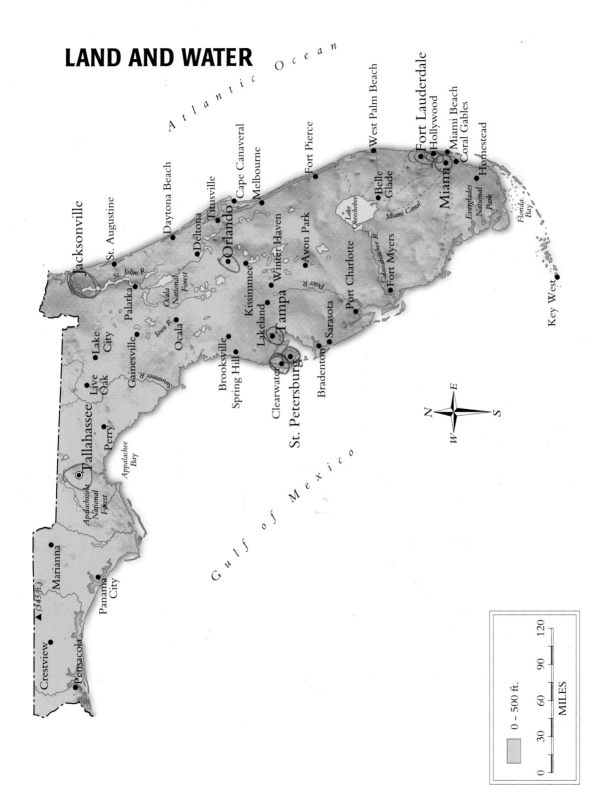

Atlantic Ocean

West Palm Beach
Fort Lauderdale
Hollywood
Miami Beach
Coral Gables
Homestead

Cape Canaveral
Melbourne
Fort Pierce
Belle
Glade
Miami Canal
Miami
Lake
Okeechobee
Everglades
National
Park
Florida
Bay

Daytona Beach
Titusville
Deltona
Orlando

Jacksonville
St. Augustine
St. Johns R.
Palatka
Ocala
National
Forest
Winter Haven
Avon Park
Caloosahatchee R.
Fort Myers
Port Charlotte
Key West

Lake
City
Gainesville
Ocala
Iowa R.
Suwannee R.
Brooksville
Spring Hill
Kissimmee
Lakeland
Tampa
Peace R.
Sarasota
Bradenton
Clearwater
St. Petersburg

Live
Oak
Tallahassee
Perry
Appalachee
Bay
Apalachicola
National
Forest
▲ (345 ft.)
Marianna
Panama
City
Crestview
Pensacola

Gulf of Mexico

N
E
S
W

0 – 500 ft.

0	30	60	90	120

MILES

elevation. The abundance of fertile soil in these areas nourishes forests of hardwood trees such as beech, holly, hickory, magnolia, maple, and oak.

Pine barrens—areas of rugged pine forests—spread out over much of central Florida. There, the dry, sandy soil is less fertile than in northern Florida, so hardwood trees are unable to grow. Instead, pine trees thrive, along with scrub oaks and palmettos.

A century ago, a large portion of Florida lay underwater at least part of the year. Today, the remaining swamps and marshland that make up the state's wetlands are concentrated in central and south Florida. The Gulf coast's saltwater marshes are an ideal habitat for mangrove trees, which have roots that thrust up out of the water. Until the recent invasion of plants from other regions, water lilies, cattails, sawgrass, bay trees, and cypress trees dominated Florida's freshwater wetlands.

The most famous stretch of Florida wetlands is the Everglades, a chain of lakes, rivers, and marshland that spreads over much of south Florida. Much of this vast wetland is made up of grasses growing up out of slow-moving water, dotted with small tree islands called hammocks. "They are, they have always been, one of the unique regions of the earth, remote, never wholly known," wrote early environmentalist Marjory Stoneman Douglas in her classic book *The Everglades: River of Grass*. "Nothing anywhere else is quite like them."

South-central Florida's Lake Okeechobee is one of the nation's largest lakes, smaller than only the Great Lakes and Utah's Great Salt Lake. It is merely the largest of the more than thirty thousand freshwater lakes and ponds in Florida.

The Everglades are "the most remarkable [region] on this continent," wrote explorer Buckingham Smith in 1848. "The water is pure and limpid and almost imperceptibly moves . . . silently and slowly to the southward."

HOLES AND REEFS

Much of the United States sits on top of granite, slate, and marble. But in Florida, limestone lies underneath the ground. That's because the ocean covered Florida more recently than the rest of the country, and the remains of sea life help form limestone. Limestone is very hard, but water carrying acid that seeps into the ground cuts holes into the stone. Over millions of years the limestone under

Florida has become filled with holes. This has allowed underwater springs and rivers to form, which feed most of Florida's rivers and lakes.

Sometimes so many holes appear in the limestone that it caves in, forming deep depressions in the earth called sinkholes. In 1981, a sinkhole that suddenly appeared in Winter Park, near Orlando, swallowed five Porsches sitting in a dealer's lot and caused $4 million damage. Sinkholes sometimes reach as deep as two hundred feet. Deep sinkholes often fill with water and become popular swimming holes. Many lakes in Florida actually sit atop sinkholes that are farther underground.

Lying underwater off the Florida coast is one of the state's most unusual geographic features—coral reefs. A coral reef is a limestone formation made up of the skeletons of millions of tiny sea creatures called polyps. Living polyps attached to these limestone bases give coral reefs their beautiful colors and extraordinary shapes, which sometime resemble fans and branches. Brightly colored tropical fish often live among the reefs, creating an exotic and lively underwater world.

The coral reefs that hug the Atlantic coastline near Miami and then wind around the Florida Keys are the only natural reefs off the continental United States. The warm Gulf Stream water flowing through the Straits of Florida nourishes these reefs.

WILDLIFE GALORE

Even after people appeared on the Florida peninsula some twelve thousand years ago, huge, now extinct animals such as woolly mammoths, mastodons, and giant tree sloths still lived there. Today, squirrels, raccoons, armadillos, opossums, deer, turtles, rabbits, otters, and gophers thrive inland. Florida panthers live primarily in the Everglades. Ordinary birds such as blue jays, vultures, crows, woodpeckers, robins, owls, geese, cardinals, and mockingbirds pepper the state.

Florida also plays at least part-time host to a range of rarer birds

"Exploring a reef is surely akin to landing on some strange planet," writer Christopher Newbert once remarked. "It is a fantastic garden . . . inhabited by strange creatures."

With its bright pink
feathers and broad, flat
bill, the roseate spoonbill
is one of Florida's most
distinctive birds.

After a swim, the anhinga
must dry out its wings
before it can fly again.

such as the lovely long-billed roseate spoonbill and the anhinga, which Floridians call the snakebird or water turkey. The anhinga puts its whole body, wings and all, into the water when it swims. Only its long curved neck and head stick out, which makes it look like a snake swimming in the water. After the bird leaves the water, it holds out its wings to dry them off. Otherwise, it would be too heavy to fly. This blow-drying pose makes the bird look like a turkey, giving rise to its other nickname.

Florida is home to many snakes that bite, but only coral snakes, certain rattlesnakes, and cottonmouths, which are also called water moccasins, are poisonous. Water moccasins hide in trees over water and can swim.

More annoying than snakes are Florida's many insects. Most homes in Florida, especially those without air conditioning, feature carefully installed screens over all the doors and windows to keep out the many bugs that thrive in the humid climate. In south Florida, it makes little sense to try to go camping any time but in the middle of winter, as mosquitoes swarm everywhere. Insect repellant can only do so much in such an environment.

Florida's most famous creature, the alligator, almost disappeared from the state at the turn of the century, when it was hunted for its skin. Now protected by law, the animal has made a big come-back in recent years. With some one million alligators now living in Florida, state officials even allow periodic gator hunting.

Visitors to Florida are most likely to see alligators when the animals are out sunning. These cold-blooded reptiles need to lay in the sun to raise their body temperature. Native Floridians can sometimes spot gators when the creatures are sitting in the mud

Although once endangered, alligators now number a million in Florida.

or water, waiting for their prey. With just its eyes, ears, and nose sticking out, a gator in this position looks like a log.

Alligators grow up to thirteen feet. They have sharp teeth and powerful tails, and they can run very quickly for short distances on land. They have no natural enemies. As Florida's alligator population rebounds and as people move farther into the creatures' natural habitat, human encounters with gators are likely to increase. Although alligators usually limit their large-animal attacks to dogs, deer, and cows, attacks on people do occur. A gator might attack a person if it is extremely hungry or if it is trying to protect its turf. "Please Don't Feed the Alligators" signs dot Florida's shores, because gators accustomed to people are more likely to attack.

In July 1986, a twenty-nine-year-old man was killed by an alligator in north Florida's Wakulla River. It was the eighth such event in Florida since 1944. The drivers of the boats that show visitors the river often joke about the possibility of such fatal encounters. In this case, when passengers caught sight of a gator dragging something underwater, the driver quipped: "Looks like he caught his lunch." The horrified passengers then realized the "lunch" was a person's body. The gator had grabbed the man, who had been swimming. It eventually left his body on the shore without eating him. Wakulla County officials shot the gator, as state law requires.

HOT AND WET

Florida's plants and animals, both dangerous and harmless, have had to adapt to the state's extreme climate. Key West is the nation's hottest city, with an average annual temperature of 77 degrees Fahrenheit. The state as a whole is very humid. South Florida barely has winter, although as recently as January 1997 a freeze took out half the area's vegetable crop. Instead, there are essentially two seasons: the wet season in summer and the dry season in winter.

North and central Florida come close to having four seasons. North Florida's hardwood forests even feature brightly colored leaves in the fall, and it occasionally snows there. But winter is still rather short, and summer is still hot. Although north Florida has notched the state's lowest recorded temperature, -2 degrees Fahrenheit in Tallahassee, it has also suffered the state's highest temperature, 109 degrees in Monticello.

Floridians are divided on the weather. "I love it," says Michigan native Barbara Knapp, now a central Florida resident. "I'm not going back . . . ever. It's too cold up there." Emily Spence Diehl, a longtime north Florida resident now living in Miami, says that she and her husband plan to move out-of-state instead of staying in south Florida. "There's no change of seasons," says Diehl. "It's really, really hot for a long time."

Florida's hot weather gives children plenty of reason to head to the pool.

Hurricane Andrew left 175,000 people homeless. Here, residents of Homestead inform friends and family that they made it through safely.

Florida suffers from more thunder, lightning, and hurricanes than any other state in the country. Hurricanes form during the late summer months when the sun heats up the moist air over the ocean and creates a rising spiral motion. These storms are shaped like giant doughnuts, with swirling winds (up to 150 miles per hour) and rain circling counterclockwise around a calm "eye" in the middle. The hurricanes that strike the continental United States form in the Caribbean and head northwest, often wreaking havoc on Florida.

In August 1992, Hurricane Andrew hit south Florida, killing dozens of people and causing $30 billion worth of damage. North Miami newcomers Clarke and Sally Campbell-Evans competed

THE WEST PALM BEACH HURRICANE

In the days before weather satellites and long-range tracking of hurricanes, these fierce tropical storms usually caught people by surprise. Despite modern advances in meteorology, the destructive force of hurricanes is still a reality, as they sweep in every fall from the Caribbean. This song is as relevant today as it was when it was written in 1928.

bo - dy got drowned in the storm.

He rode out on the ocean,
Chained the lightning to his wheel,
Stepped on land at West Palm Beach,
And the wicked hearts did yield.
Chorus

Over in Pahokee,
Families rushed out at the door,
And somebody's poor mother
Haven't been seen anymore.
Chorus

Some mothers looked at their children,
As they began to cry,
Cried, "Lord, have mercy,
For we all must die."
Chorus

I tell you wicked people,
What you had better do;
Go down and get the Holy Ghost
And then you live the life, too.
Chorus

Out around Okeechobee,
All scattered on the ground,
The last account of the dead they had
Were twenty-two hundred found.
Chorus

South Bay, Belleglade, and Pahokee,
Tell me they all went down,
And over at Chosen,
Everybody got drowned.
Chorus

Some people are yet missing,
And they haven't been found, they say.
But this we know, they will come forth
On the Resurrection Day.
Chorus

When Gabriel sounds the trumpet,
and the dead begin to rise,
I'll meet the saints from Chosen,
Up in the heavenly skies.
Chorus

with their neighbors for supplies such as batteries at the supermarket the night before the storm. But they never got to watch the eight videos they rented, because they were without electricity for more than a week. "We were pretty stupid," says Sally Campbell-Evans. "We had never lived through one."

Florida's recent hurricanes have caused long-term economic problems, as coastal development has slowed and insurance costs have soared. But hurricanes such as Andrew also leave psychological damage. For instance, they cause divorce and suicide rates to rise.

DRAINING THE EVERGLADES

As dangerous as Florida's natural environment can be, it has also proven vulnerable. The state, once an unspoiled subtropical paradise, has quickly acquired more than its share of environmental problems. Rapid population growth is primarily to blame. "So many people are coming here, they're killing the things they came to see," says north Florida journalist Julie Hauserman.

The catastrophic effects of the state's ever-increasing population are most evident in south Florida. There, human intervention now threatens the very existence of the Everglades.

Until the twentieth century, water from central Florida flowed southward into the Kissimmee River, Lake Okeechobee, and then through the Everglades National Park into Florida Bay at the southern tip of the peninsula. In the 1960s, the government eliminated the bends in the Kissimmee River, turning it into a straight-line ditch. They built a hundred-mile-long dike around Lake Okeechobee, as well as canals from the lake to the area's

MYSTERIOUS TRIANGLE

Some Floridians are not content to worry about alligators and hurricanes and the other real dangers posed by Florida's environment. Instead, they are fascinated by the mysteries of the so-called Devil's Triangle or Bermuda Triangle, an area of the Atlantic Ocean between southeast Florida, Puerto Rico, and Bermuda. They believe this area has experienced an abnormally high number of unexplained boat and plane accidents.

One of the most famous Devil's Triangle incidents occurred in 1945, when all five navy bomber planes on a training mission were lost. None of the fourteen crew members were ever found.

No one is certain what happened, but Devil's Triangle enthusiasts have come up with some imaginative answers. Some have suggested that aliens kidnapped the crew to study humans. Others have speculated that a giant sea monster, a mysterious time-space warp, or an undersea power source from the Lost Continent of Atlantis disturbs magnetic and electrical fields, causing the area's many accidents.

Government officials deny that the region suffers from an unusual number of accidents and disappearances. They blame the incidents on heavy traffic, pilot and boater inexperience, magnetic abnormalities that limit compass effectiveness, shifting sandbars, high winds, and poor tracking of aircraft. "All of these so-called mysteries are not mysteries at all," says Josh McDowell, an oceanographer with Miami's National Hurricane Center.

rivers. As a result, water that used to flow slowly south through the Everglades into Florida Bay now flows either directly east into the Atlantic or west into the Gulf of Mexico. This drained the area south of the lake, turning it into some of the world's richest

When the meandering 90-mile Kissimmee River was converted into a straight 52-mile canal, nearby plants died, the bird population fell, and wetlands along its banks dried into pastures.

agricultural land. Draining these wetlands also made room for suburban development in the area.

It is now clear that the authorities did too good a job of drying out the Everglades. Rainwater flows so quickly to the Atlantic and the gulf today that little remains for the slow flow southward. As a result, the Everglades dries out more than ever during the dry season. This means that wildfires rage more frequently in the wintertime, and that fragile native plants are being crowded out by hardier plants from other parts of the world, which are better able to survive under dry conditions. South Florida, one of the wettest areas of the country historically, now suffers from water shortages.

Scientists have discovered that wetlands and winding rivers such as the Kissimmee help the environment because they curb flooding and purify water naturally. Today, authorities are engaged in a $346 million effort to try to undo what they did to the Kissimmee in the 1960s. To restore the bends in the river, they are building the banks of the river back up, forcing the water to snake around as it did before.

The agricultural and suburban development that accompanied the draining of the wetlands caused other problems as well. The presence of so many people and crops has encouraged insect-killing efforts, which spread pesticides throughout the state. Scientists fear that these pesticides will eventually enter Florida's underground water supply, killing fish and threatening the quality of the state's drinking water.

The introduction of exotic plants from faraway lands has wreaked havoc on the state's environment. Frequently these plants have no natural enemies in Florida, and they quickly elbow out native plants. Authorities trying to drain Florida's wetlands introduced melaleuca into the Everglades. This sponge-like tree is now spreading like wildfire, speeding up the drying of the Everglades.

Another cause of environmental concern is the fertilizer used in farming and on lawns. Farmers feed cattle phosphorous as a nutrient. When cow manure laced with phosphorous settles in

THE GENTLE GIANT

Of all the creatures threatened by the development of Florida's wetlands, the most beloved is the West Indian manatee. Roughly three thousand manatees live in Florida's waters today. These huge, slow mammals eat as much as a hundred pounds of plants each day and sometimes weigh 3,500 pounds.

The manatees' habitat is continually shrinking because of drainage and development. But boats pose the most immediate danger to the animals. Because manatees are slow and must surface to breathe, motorboats speeding through the water often hit them or cut them with their propellers. As a result, propeller marks frequently scar the manatees' gray, leathery skin. "They're big, cuddly, dumb animals that are really innocently getting slaughtered," says Greg Diehl, who once worked for Florida's manatee protection program.

lakes, however, it can speed the growth of algae, which threatens to choke lakes. This has started to happen in Lake Okeechobee.

PROTECTING THE ENVIRONMENT

In recent years, Floridians have voted for several controversial conservation measures, which major industries opposed. These laws limit the size of nets commercial fishing operations can use and require polluters of the Everglades—primarily the sugar industry—to pay for cleaning up the area. In Florida's most successful conservation initiative, the state government has bought up huge tracts of land to save it from development.

Because Florida's tourism and fishing industries depend on a healthy environment, these powerful groups sometimes side with environmentalists. In northwest Florida, the fishing industry helped keep oil drilling from most of the Gulf coast.

Florida's beautiful natural environment is still the envy of many northerners. With the cooperation of industry, as well as heightened conservation efforts and better regulation of the state's explosive growth, perhaps Floridians will be able to preserve what remains of Florida's unique landscape.

2 BECOMING FLORIDA

Landscape with Heron *by Herman Herzog*

The first Floridians made their way to the region roughly twelve thousand years ago. These were the ancestors of the people we now call Native Americans. The newcomers managed to adapt to Florida's hot, sticky climate. Luckily, the area had many food sources. The first Floridians hunted, fished, and gathered shellfish. By the time Europeans arrived in the region, Florida's Native Americans were growing crops such as corn.

NATIVE AMERICAN LIFE

At that time, three major Native American cultures—the Apalachee in the northwest, the Timucua in the northeast, and the Calusa in the southwest—were spread out over Florida. Although these groups apparently spoke different languages and clashed regularly, they shared some cultural elements.

Florida's Native American groups were ruled by chieftains and religious leaders. Villages were arranged around the chieftain's house and the council buildings where assemblies met. Most houses were made with small branches woven together and then covered with mud and clay. The roofs were thatched with palm leaves.

Most Native Americans in the area engaged in an annual ritual dance that sometimes lasted several days. During this time, they drank a harsh black tea made from holly leaves. Although the

When Spanish explorer Juan Ponce de León landed near present-day Cape Canaveral in 1513, he dubbed the region La Florida, *"the flowery land."*

tea made them vomit, it was intended to purify their mind and spirit.

MEETING THE EUROPEANS

Spanish explorers were the first Europeans to make contact with Florida's Native Americans. A fleet sailing from Puerto Rico under Juan Ponce de León landed in Florida in 1513. Either because of the land's flowery appearance or because he landed around Easter, which was known as *Pascua Florida*, or "Feast of the Flowers," de León dubbed the peninsula La Florida. De León and a series of Spanish expeditions under Panfilo de Narváez, Hernando de Soto, and Pedro de Menéndez de Avilés were looking for precious metals, but they also tried to conquer the land and its people.

AN EXPLORER'S JOURNAL

Álvar Núñez Cabeza de Vaca was one of four survivors of an ill-fated Spanish expedition into Florida. In July 1528, after looting the grain supply of Native Americans in north Florida, the expedition headed for Apalachicola Bay. In his classic account of the journey, Cabeza de Vaca wrote admiringly of the Indians' skill with bow and arrows:

Good armor did no good against arrows in this skirmish. There were men who swore they had seen two red oaks, each the thickness of a man's calf, pierced from side to side by arrows this day; which is no wonder when you consider the power and skill the Indians can deliver them with. I myself saw an arrow buried half a foot in a poplar tree.

All the Indians we had so far seen in Florida had been archers. They loomed big and naked and from a distance looked like giants. They were handsomely proportioned, lean, agile, and strong. Their bows were as thick as an arm, six or seven feet long, accurate at twenty paces.

Thanks to Florida's rough environment and the Spaniards' supply problems and weakening empire back in Europe, all these expeditions failed. Menéndez, however, did establish a settlement at St. Augustine in northeast Florida, in 1565. This is the oldest permanent European settlement in the United States.

In the long run, the arrival of the Spanish decimated the Native American population for reasons that had nothing to do with warfare. Travel had exposed Europeans to most of the world's diseases. But the isolated Native Americans had never faced many of the diseases the Europeans brought with them to the Americas, so their bodies had no natural resistance to them. Florida's Native American population dropped from 350,000 to 1,000 in the two centuries following Ponce de León's arrival. "Their whole social structure was completely uprooted by disease," says historian David Proctor. "They lost faith in their religion. They were totally beaten down."

Soon after the first explorers landed in Florida, Spanish priests came to the region to try to convert the Indians to Christianity. Sometimes the Native Americans were killed if they refused. Ravaged by disease and impressed by the Spaniards' military might, Native American leaders eventually invited Spanish priests to live among them in their villages. Many Native Americans converted to Catholicism, at least outwardly. Eventually, several dozen Spanish missions dotted the north Florida landscape.

In addition to Native Americans and Spaniards, Florida was home to many African Americans. The Spanish brought Africans to Florida as slaves. Many free blacks, some of whom had escaped from slavery in other colonies, also lived in the area. Compared to other parts of what would become the United States, Spanish Florida developed a less rigid attitude toward racial separation. Intermarriage, or at least child-bearing, among Spaniards, Native Americans, and African Americans was common.

This relatively peaceful society lasted less than a century before being destroyed by people to the north. The British were colonizing Georgia, and they eventually joined forces with the Creek, a Native American group in the area, and began pressing south.

The Spaniards had built an impressive fort, the *Castillo de San*

St. Augustine, the headquarters of Spanish Florida, is the oldest European settlement in the United States.

Marcos, at their St. Augustine headquarters. It was made of a mixture of mud and crushed seashells, a substance that the Spanish dubbed *coquina* (pronounced koh-KEE-nah). Twice in the early 1700s, the British attacked St. Augustine. The Spaniards and their Native American and African-American allies survived these assaults because the coquina was so soft that the fort's thick walls absorbed British cannonballs without crumbling.

But the Creek continued to raid Florida, and Florida's Native

Americans kept dying. Soon they had virtually vanished. Meanwhile, the Spanish were weakening and had only enough resources to maintain small military bases in St. Augustine and Pensacola. To hold onto Florida, the Spanish encouraged other Native American groups—mainly Creek and Yamassee from Georgia and the Carolinas—to resettle the area. This hybrid group became known as the "Seminole," which means something like "runaway" or "outlaw," although historians disagree about whether the word comes from Spanish or a Native American language. These new Floridians adopted many of the customs of the area's earlier Native Americans, including the ritual dance, the black tea, and rule by chieftains.

THE RISE OF ANDREW JACKSON

Although Native Americans allied with the Spanish resettled much of Florida, Spain never regained any effective control there. "Vast swaths of Florida were totally unpoliced by any authority," says historian David Proctor. From the mid-1780s on, some African Americans fleeing slavery in Georgia and Alabama began living with Florida's Native Americans, becoming black Seminoles. Meanwhile, white Georgians, eyeing Florida lands, engaged in a series of skirmishes with the Native Americans and African Americans already in Florida. These battles eventually gave rise to the First Seminole War.

The commander of U.S. troops in this undeclared war was General Andrew Jackson. Throughout his career in Florida, Jackson ruthlessly pursued his goal of removing to the west the Native Americans he did not kill.

In the 1830s, some Seminole retreated deep into the Everglades to avoid being forced out of Florida.

In 1817, a group of African Americans took over the so-called Negro Fort at Prospect Bluffs along northwest Florida's Apalachicola River. They blocked illegal U.S. shipping down the Apalachicola. Taking advantage of Southern white's fears of armed blacks, General Jackson easily raised a militia in southern Georgia. This unit killed 270 blacks stationed at the fort with a lucky cannon shot to the powder magazine.

Jackson's troops then pillaged northern Florida. They re-enslaved the African Americans living in the area and forced the Seminoles into central and southern Florida. In 1821, Spain, which had long been powerless in Florida despite its official control of the territory, ceded all of Florida to the United States. Jackson became Florida's first territorial governor.

White people soon descended on the new U.S. territory. Some were wealthy planters from Georgia and the Carolinas, who moved south with their families and slaves. They began growing cotton in the five-county area around Tallahassee, the new territorial capital. This region soon gained the trappings of the Old South, with its cotton fields, large estates, plantation houses, Spanish moss, magnolia trees, and black-majority populations. Because of the nearby bend around the Gulf of Mexico, this cotton plantation area became known as the Big Bend.

Poorer white families moved into the rest of north Florida. These hardy pioneers raised beef cattle, tapped pine trees for turpentine, chopped down trees to sell to timber mills, trapped raccoons for their furs, and hunted, fished, and grew vegetables for food. Some found the rugged lifestyle too difficult, and returned north or moved out west. Others stuck with it. "The main thing was to live their own lives, to live off the land," says librarian Frank Mendola.

A GUERRILLA WAR

Land-hungry whites soon began penetrating the central Florida area that treaties had set aside for the Seminoles. This tense situation continued until two leaders emerged who pushed the U.S. government and Native Americans into a bloody, seven-year-long guerrilla war.

Andrew Jackson was committed to removing all Native Americans from Florida.

Osceola by George Catlin. Osceola refused to sign away any Seminole lands. At one treaty conference he stabbed his knife into a document, exclaiming "The only treaty I will ever make is this!"

Leading the U.S. side was the Seminoles' old nemesis Andrew Jackson, who had been elected U.S. president in 1828. Jackson was committed to removing all Native Americans from Florida. "I tell you that you must go and that you will go," he declared. Leading the Native Americans was Osceola, a fiery former Creek with at least two white ancestors. Osceola adamantly opposed Jackson's order, and he was ready to fight for what he believed in. His aggressiveness enabled him to usurp the power of the traditional, hereditary Seminole chiefs.

Despite Osceola's efforts, an act of treachery eventually ensured U.S. victory in the war. Under a white flag of truce, a group of Seminole leaders including Osceola approached the camp of General Thomas Jesup, the commander of the U.S. troops in Florida at the time. But once the leaders were in custody, Jesup ignored the flag. The general threw Osceola and the others into prison in the old Castillo de San Marcos. Sick and exhausted, Osceola died in a South Carolina fort in 1838.

Three hundred Seminoles fled into the Everglades to avoid going out west. The U.S. government fought a third Seminole war in the 1850s to ship out all but a hundred of them. With this, a sad, bloody chapter in Florida's history had ended.

THE CIVIL WAR

Florida entered the Union as a slave state in March 1845 in a deal between Northerners and Southerners in which a free state, Iowa, was admitted the same year. When the Civil War broke out in 1861, white Floridians allied with other white Southerners to defend slavery. Florida was not the scene of major fighting. Instead, the state's importance lay in its contribution of salt, beef, and soldiers to the losing Confederate effort.

After the war, Floridians had difficulty rebuilding the state and incorporating the newly freed blacks into society on an equal basis with whites. White and black proponents of this effort, known as Reconstruction, fought among themselves. Only one African American, Jonathan Gibbs, gained statewide office, serving as Florida's secretary of state and superintendent of public instruction. Florida Democrats, united in their opposition to Reconstruction, helped end the effort—in Florida and across the South—in 1876.

In the following two decades, Florida legislators passed laws

Jonathan C. Gibbs, the only African-American Floridian to gain statewide office during Reconstruction, served as Florida's superintendent of public instruction and secretary of state.

making it impossible for Florida's blacks to participate in government or mingle as equals with whites. Laws required each adult who wanted to vote to pay a tax, which many African Americans could not afford. In Florida, the Democratic Party soon dominated state politics, and Democrats banned blacks from the all-important Democratic primary, which settled most elections. By the turn of the century, laws kept blacks and whites from marrying, attending school together, or sitting together on buses. Custom kept blacks and whites from dining together or shaking hands. This separation of blacks and whites was known as segregation.

Segregation kept many African Americans in terror and poverty, but it did have one positive side effect. Because blacks could not eat in the same restaurants as whites or shop in the same stores, they started their own restaurants and businesses. Soon, many Florida cities had thriving black business districts. Miami's black neighborhood of Overtown featured an entertainment district that became known as Little Broadway. In the 1920s and 1930s, the African-American pioneers of jazz and blues often stayed and performed there.

TOURISM AND TECHNOLOGY

While many leaders in turn-of-the-century Florida were busy establishing segregation, others were working with northern businessmen for a different cause: Florida's economic growth and development. Northerners Henry Flagler and Henry Plant built railroads and beautiful hotels up and down the state. Frequently, the same trains that brought tourists into the state carried out

Early trains bringing tourists to Florida sometimes stopped to allow the visitors to pick citrus fruit.

citrus fruit, an increasingly important Florida farm product.

Promoters marketing the state as a tourist and retirement mecca helped spur a massive real estate boom in south Florida in the 1920s. Up north, people heard about the fabulous money to be made as land prices shot through the roof. A New York man went to Florida with $1,000 and returned three weeks later with $375,000. In 1925, two men bought a stretch of beach near Miami for $3 million and sold it two days later for $7.5 million. A week later it was sold again for $42 million.

People streamed down the Dixie Highway into Florida in order to

During the south Florida real estate boom in 1925, auctioneers scrambled atop cars to sell land to the 2.5 million people who poured into the state.

get in on the action. Shady businessmen hawked land on roadsides and street corners. During the height of the boom, a British visitor wrote, "It was a common sight at any wayside barbecue on the Dixie Highway to see some purple-faced orator mounted on the back seat of his car under the blazing sun bellowing of the land of hope to an awestruck audience standing around him." Often, these men were peddling swampland to unsuspecting Northerners.

By 1926, the madness had subsided. Land prices plummeted, and many people were left in financial ruin. A devastating hurricane that September killed nearly four hundred people. Two years later, another hurricane hit, killing about two thousand people. In 1929, the Great Depression descended upon the entire country. There was no question then that the boom was over.

Despite the emerging tourist trade, in 1940 Florida was still the most rural, sparsely populated Southern state and only the twenty-seventh most populous state in the country. In fifty short years, it became the South's most urban state and the nation's fourth most populous. This was possible because of the rise of several technologies that made it easier to live year-round in central and south Florida.

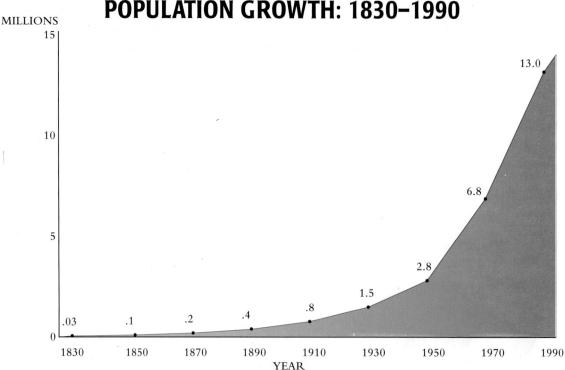

POPULATION GROWTH: 1830–1990

In the 1840s, North Florida doctor John Gorrie, a mayor of Apalachicola, had invented the basic technology for air conditioning and refrigeration as a way to treat his malaria patients. Later innovators perfected the technology. Air conditioning became widely available in the 1950s. First it was used to cool movie theaters, then other public buildings, and finally private homes. By the 1970s, most middle-class Floridians could move from their air-conditioned home to their air-conditioned car to their air-conditioned office, often without breaking a sweat, even in 99-degree heat.

Other technologies also fueled the state's growth. Drainage and insect control made the state a more comfortable place to live. The development of inexpensive cars made it possible for middle-class families to visit Florida as tourists. Airplanes eased visits by people from around the world. Both trucks and planes also sped the delivery of Florida farm products to distant markets.

"Industrialization and the mass production of automobiles led to the '20s real estate boom in Miami," says David Proctor. "Really, from then on, it's just the same old story—the real estate boom, the leisure. It just spread all over the state."

By the 1950s, tourism had really taken hold in Florida. Central Florida's Cypress Gardens and northeast Florida's Marineland, a forerunner of Sea World, led the way. Entertainers such as Arthur Godfrey and Jackie Gleason broadcast television shows from Miami Beach, which helped attract tourists to the region. Northern college students began spending spring break on the Fort Lauderdale beaches, and later, Daytona Beach and Panama City Beach.

The Land of Palms and Sunshine

MIAMI
By the Sea

Winter Tourist Season
November to May
Famous Band Concerts-December to April

Florida has been enticing tourists with its mild winters since the early twentieth century.

THE CIVIL RIGHTS MOVEMENT

Although Florida was becoming increasingly prosperous and populated, blacks still suffered widespread discrimination. Beginning in the late 1940s, Harry T. Moore led a movement in Florida to register African Americans to vote. He also encouraged black teachers to sue for salaries equal to those of their white counterparts. But Moore's work did not escape the attention of white racists. On Christmas night, 1951, whites firebombed Moore's central Florida home, killing him and his wife. But the voter-registration effort spearheaded by Moore was successful enough that by 1960 a higher proportion of blacks were registered to vote in Florida than in all but one other state.

In the late 1950s and early 1960s, Floridians, like people throughout the South, were trying to desegregate buses, restaurants, and motels. In Tallahassee, two African-American college students were arrested for sitting in a "whites only" section of a bus. A young black minister, C. K. Steele, led a boycott of the bus company and became part of the influential national network of civil rights leaders associated with Dr. Martin Luther King Jr.

In 1964, activists threatened Florida's tourist industry by trying to desegregate public beaches, swimming pools, and motels. They targeted St. Augustine in the midst of its celebration of the three hundredth anniversary of the Spanish settlement of the city. As blacks descended on the "whites only" beaches and pools, white civil rights foes also crowded the city. State officials failed to keep the peace, and the headlines about violence at the St. Augustine "swim-ins" helped push Congress to pass the Civil Rights Act, which banned discrimination at public accommodations.

Throughout the twentieth century, more and more people moved to Florida from all over the United States and every corner of the world, including a large Hispanic population. Incorporating these diverse peoples has not always been easy. As the state has prospered, Floridians have had to work harder to maintain the way of life that drew people there in the first place.

3 WORKING TOGETHER

The capitol in Tallahassee

Florida's warm climate has been crucial to the state's economy, which depends heavily on tourism, agriculture, and military spending. It has also caused millions of new residents and tourists to descend upon the state in search of balmy weather and beautiful beaches. The state government, however, has not always been able to deal with the consequences of this rapid growth.

INSIDE GOVERNMENT

Florida's state government has three branches: executive, legislative, and judicial. In this way it resembles the federal government and other state governments. But the balance of power among the three branches is somewhat unusual in Florida.

Executive. Florida's governor appoints upper-level state court judges, submits an annual budget to the legislature, signs and vetoes bills, and runs cabinet meetings. Despite these many powers, Florida's governor is relatively weak. He or she runs only half of the state government agencies. Six other officials run the rest, either as individuals or collectively with the governor as the cabinet. The governor also can serve only two consecutive four-year terms.

Legislative. Florida's legislature passes laws and budgets and proposes changes to the state constitution. The legislature is composed of two chambers. The House of Representatives has 120

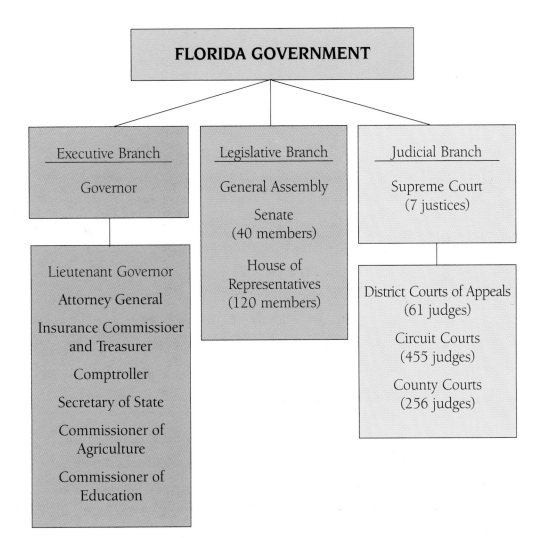

FLORIDA GOVERNMENT

Executive Branch

Governor

Lieutenant Governor

Attorney General

Insurance Commissioer
and Treasurer

Comptroller

Secretary of State

Commissioner of
Agriculture

Commissioner of
Education

Legislative Branch

General Assembly

Senate
(40 members)

House of
Representatives
(120 members)

Judicial Branch

Supreme Court
(7 justices)

District Courts of Appeals
(61 judges)

Circuit Courts
(455 judges)

County Courts
(256 judges)

members who serve two-year terms, while the Florida Senate has 40 members who serve four-year terms. Starting in the year 2000, legislators will only be able to serve eight consecutive years.

Florida has one of the most powerful state legislatures in the country. Legislative leaders often ignore the governor's budget recommendations and come up with their own figures.

Judicial. Four levels of courts make up the state court system. County courts deal with misdemeanor charges and small lawsuits.

The state's twenty circuit courts deal with felony charges and larger lawsuits. Judges on these courts are elected by Florida's voters.

Lower court decisions may be appealed to Florida's district courts of appeal and then to the Florida supreme court. Death penalty appeals and cases involving state or federal constitutional questions can go directly to this high court. Judges on these higher courts are appointed by the governor. But governors cannot just appoint whomever they want. Instead, the governor must choose from a list of three names supplied by the Judicial Nominating Committee.

In Florida, the courts are generally the most liberal branch of state government. Over the years, they have proven perfectly willing to declare actions by the governor or legislature unconstitutional.

FARMING AND MINING

Agriculture has fueled much of Florida's economic development. Draining the Everglades uncovered some fantastically rich soil, permitting the development of sugarcane fields south of Lake Okeechobee. It also helped turn the area southwest of Miami into the winter vegetable capital of the country.

Today, Florida is the nation's top producer of sugarcane. Florida trails only California in the production of fresh vegetables such as tomatoes, corn, beans, and peppers. Beef and dairy cattle also play an important role in Florida's economy, making up roughly a quarter of the state's farm income.

Florida produces much of the nation's citrus fruit and the vast majority of its orange juice. Citrus groves once dotted much of Florida, but freezing weather and suburban development elimi-

EARNING A LIVING

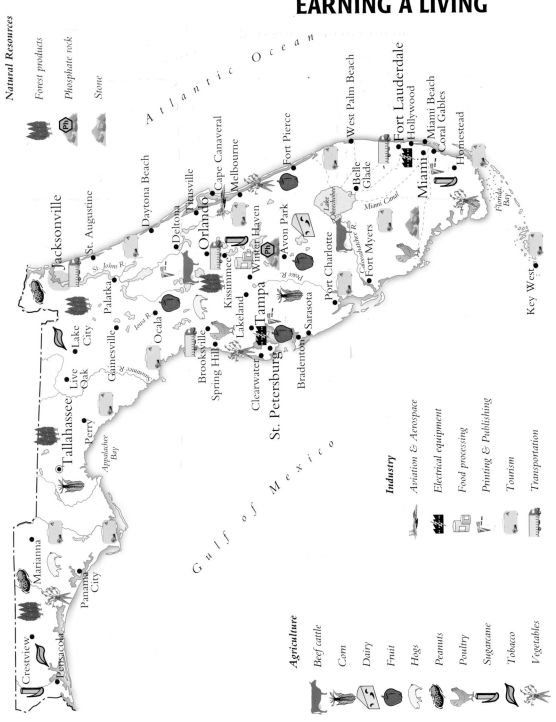

Natural Resources

Forest products

Phosphate rock

Stone

Industry

Aviation & Aerospace

Electrical equipment

Food processing

Printing & Publishing

Tourism

Transportation

Agriculture

Beef cattle

Corn

Dairy

Fruit

Hogs

Peanuts

Poultry

Sugarcane

Tobacco

Vegetables

Atlantic Ocean

Gulf of Mexico

West Palm Beach
Fort Lauderdale
Hollywood
Miami Beach
Coral Gables
Homestead
Miami

Belle
Glade

Miami Canal

Florida
Bay

Key West

Fort Pierce

Cape Canaveral
Melbourne

Titusville
Deltona
Orlando

Winter Haven
Kissimmee

Lake
Okeechobee

Caloosahatchee R.
Fort Myers

Port Charlotte

Peace R.

Avon Park

Ph

Daytona Beach

Jacksonville

St. Augustine

Palatka
St. Johns R.

Gainesville

Ocala
Iowa R.

Lake
City

Live
Oak

Suwannee R.

Brooksville
Spring Hill

Lakeland

Tampa

Clearwater
St. Petersburg

Bradenton
Sarasota

Tallahassee
Perry

Appalachee
Bay

Crestview
Pensacola

Marianna

Panama
City

Oranges are Florida's biggest crop.

nated many of the ones in north Florida. Today, citrus groves are concentrated in the south-central part of the state.

Some eighty-five thousand farmworkers in Florida toil at such dirty, difficult jobs as chopping sugarcane and picking fruit. Until the middle of the twentieth century, Florida farmworkers were generally African-American or Mexican-American. Today, most are recent immigrants from Haiti, Nicaragua, El Salvador, Guatemala, and Vietnam. They are very vulnerable to being mistreated, says farmworker organizer Tirso Moreno, because "they don't know

English, they don't know the laws, and they have no relatives here." These farmworkers face long hours, low pay, frequent on-the-job accidents, and possible pesticide exposure.

Phosphate, which farmers feed to cattle and use to fertilize plants, is the state's only important mining industry. Florida produces about four-fifths of the nation's phosphate supply, and about a quarter of the world's.

Most Florida farmworkers are immigrants who sometimes perform such backbreaking tasks as harvesting sugarcane.

1992 GROSS STATE PRODUCT: $222.6 BILLION

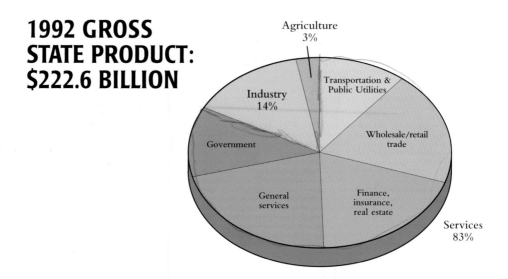

Agriculture
3%

Transportation &
Public Utilities

Industry
14%

Wholesale/retail
trade

Government

General
services

Finance,
insurance,
real estate

Services
83%

MICKEY MANIA

The same warm, sunny weather that helped make Florida an agricultural wonderland also attracted tourists to the state. Although Miami Beach was already a tourist mecca in the 1950s, the Florida tourist economy didn't reach high gear until the arrival of Walt Disney World in 1971.

When Walt Disney and his brother, Roy, were looking for potential sites for a new theme park complex, they considered Niagara Falls, St. Louis, and the Great Smoky Mountains. But none of these places could beat central Florida's great weather, open land, and cheap real estate. So the Disney brothers settled on a huge tract of wetlands and orange groves southwest of Orlando.

Some forty thousand Floridians now work at Disney World, trying to entertain thirty million visitors a year. "We want our guests to feel that when they come on to the Walt Disney World property, they've left the real world behind, they've left behind their cares and

Tourism is vital to Florida's economy. Walt Disney World is the state's number one attraction.

worries, and they're here to have a good time," says Barbara Knapp, a Disney personnel manager.

Disney World helped make central Florida one of the nation's leading tourist destinations. Today, it is just a part of Florida's booming tourist industry. More than forty million people visit Florida every year. In 1994, tourism pumped over $30 billion into the Florida economy.

AIRPLANES AND ROCKETS

Florida's warm weather and flat land have also encouraged the growth of the state's military industries, because they make ideal conditions for training pilots. Florida was awash with military training activity during World War II. A huge training facility called Camp Blanding was built in northeast Florida. Northwest Florida became the site of Eglin Air Force Base, the world's largest. Soldiers trained for the D-Day invasion of Europe during World War II on the Gulf beaches of the Big Bend's Camp Gordon Johnson. By the end of the war, forty military air bases were strewn throughout Florida.

In the following decades, the American government's concern about possible conflicts with Cuba ensured that the military would continue to expand in Florida. Today, Tampa's Special Operations Center directs major U.S. military operations, such as the Persian Gulf War. Even with budget cuts, some sixty thousand military personnel work in Florida, more than in all but five other states.

An important outgrowth of the military presence in Florida has been the state's aerospace economy. In 1950, Cape Canaveral, on the Atlantic coast in central Florida, became the home of the U.S.

With sixty thousand military personnel stationed in Florida, the state has seen many difficult good-byes.

space program in part because of its good weather and seaside location. This program has had some tremendous successes. In 1969, it landed Apollo 11 on the moon, and it now routinely sends space shuttles into orbit. At its high point, before budget cuts struck, the space program employed twenty thousand central Floridians; now it employs roughly thirteen thousand.

Manufacturing plays a relatively minor role in the Florida economy. Paper mills, phosphate plants, and juice plants provide much of the employment in some rural Florida counties. But most of the state's half million factory workers are employed in big cities such as Jacksonville, Miami, and Tampa.

WITNESSING THE CHALLENGER EXPLOSION

Disasters have periodically struck the space program. These tragedies have affected the Floridians who work for the program as much as anyone.

Kurt Eichin's father worked on the space program, and Eichin grew up wanting to be an astronaut. In January 1986, Eichin stood outside his Daytona apartment to watch the launch of the space shuttle *Challenger*. "I saw it go up, and I saw the explosion," says Eichin. "I kept waiting." Eichin figured the shuttle, if it had a problem, would just fly back to the Space Center. But the shuttle did not reappear out of the smoke. "I immediately called my Dad, and I said, 'Dad, tell me that didn't just happen.' He said, 'We all knew it was going to happen some day. It happened today.'"

Cold weather and a defective part had apparently caused the explosion at forty-six thousand feet. Searchers never found the bodies of the seven crew members, including school-teacher Christa McAuliffe.

"I was stunned, just absolutely stunned," says Eichin. "I cried. I just couldn't believe it. The space program had been my whole family's bread and butter. This was an incredible failure of the whole system."

Witnessing the disaster hasn't dimmed Eichin's enthusiasm for the space program, however. Says Eichin: "I'd still love to be an astronaut."

Miami has become an important center in the worldwide economy and is the site of the Latin American headquarters of many major corporations.

Florida's location has helped it become a major center of international trade and finance. Today, Florida boasts several major ports, and most of the cruise ships that ply the Caribbean operate out of south Florida ports. Miami, the city dubbed the Capital of the Caribbean, boasts one of the nation's busiest airports. Banking, finance, and insurance have also become increasingly important parts of Florida's urban economy.

TOO MANY PEOPLE

Economic growth during the last fifty years has fueled a rapid rise in Florida's population. But Florida is no longer among the nation's fastest-growing states. The most obvious reasons for this are the state's increasingly heavy traffic and congestion, and its high crime rate. These make it a less attractive place for new residents and businesses and eventually drive away some people who have moved to the state. The problems have grown worse because Florida's state government has had trouble managing and coping with growth.

Florida has the third-highest rate of deaths in car accidents in the country. In Miami drivers spend more time on the road than drivers in all but three other Southern cities, and five of the top fifteen most congested Southern cities are in Florida.

The roots of these problems lie in the character of Florida's rapid development. Florida suffers from urban sprawl—the development of sparsely populated, far-flung suburbs. Urban sprawl lengthens drives between work, home, and shopping and discourages the development of mass transit.

A 1980s effort to require new residents and developers to build and pay for roads and public services *before* the need for them arises has fallen apart. As urban sprawl and poor planning continue, so do congestion and traffic accidents.

CRIME AND KIDS

Florida has the highest crime rate of any state in the country and is home to the city with the highest crime rate—Miami. Only New York state arrests more teenagers for committing violent crimes.

People don't agree on exactly what causes the state's crime problem. Some people stress the social problems that can

A quarter of Florida's children grow up in poor families.

contribute to crime. They point out that workers often earn low wages, and as a result, a quarter of Florida children grow up in poor families. Florida's tax and welfare systems are also hard on poor families, and Florida spends a relatively modest amount on schools. "They've cheated kids for a very long time in this state," says Mary Gonzalez, head of the Tampa area teachers' union.

Other people argue that Florida's crime problem is at least partially the result of a breakdown in families. They say that parents are not teaching their children morals or disciplining them.

Still other people believe that the state has been letting convicted criminals out of jail too easily. For many years, rather than spending the money to build new prisons if the old ones were full, the state released convicts early. Many inmates out on parole then committed more crimes.

The whole world heard about Florida's crime problem in the early 1990s. Twice in one year serial killers struck Gainesville, usually a quiet university town. Florida also suffered a rash of crimes against foreign tourists. Carjackings became a problem in Miami, and a British tourist sleeping at a north Florida rest area was killed in a botched robbery. The details of this murder underline Florida's problem with troubled kids and easy probation: the apparent ringleader was a thirteen-year-old boy whom police had already arrested more than fifty times.

Floridians at a gun buyback give cash for weapons, no questions asked, in an attempt to stem the state's high rate of violent crime.

FACING THE MUSIC

Faced with this highly publicized crime problem, Florida acted more aggressively than it has against congestion and environmental problems. The courts began sentencing teenagers convicted of crimes more strictly, and the state built more prisons so adult convicts now spend most of their sentences in prison, instead of out on parole. Florida also executes convicted killers at a higher rate than all but one other state.

Florida has also taken some steps to address the social problems that contribute to crime. It has improved access to health care for poor families with children and is experimenting with allowing community groups to run special public schools, which students can choose to attend instead of regular public schools.

Florida will undoubtedly continue to face problems such as crime and congestion in the years to come. If these problems are allowed to fester, they could very well halt the growth that has transformed the state in the past half century. But most Floridians don't want that. They hope instead to find more creative ways to guide growth and reduce the problems that it sometimes breeds.

4 CULTURAL CROSSROADS

Florida is made up of people from all over the world. But this rich diversity has sometimes divided people along cultural, economic, religious, and regional lines. When Florida became a state, rich Episcopalian planters, poor evangelical Protestant farmers, African-American slaves, and Native Americans made up the population. Today, many other groups have added to the mix.

MOVING SOUTH

Northern immigrants began arriving in Florida after the Civil War. By the turn of the century, the nation's new wealthy elite were flooding into southeast Florida, the so-called Gold Coast. Some of the richest families in the country still live in Palm Beach and Boca Raton and across the peninsula in Naples.

In recent decades, older people of all different backgrounds have moved from the Northeast and Midwest to central and south Florida, turning the state into a retirement haven. Many retirees return north for half the year, avoiding Florida's hot summers. Floridians call these folks snowbirds. "As we get older, we like to have a warm climate," says Reverend Harley Martin, an Ohio native who now lives most of the year in Avon Park.

Native white Floridians have often been ambivalent about these Northern migrants. Even today, some Floridians use "Yankee" as an insult.

So many retired people have moved to Florida that it now has the highest percentage of senior citizens of any state.

AFRICAN AMERICANS TODAY

Civil rights struggles gripped Florida in the 1950s and 1960s. Today, issues such as welfare dependency, crime, and housing segregation divide many of Florida's blacks and whites. Per capita income for Florida's blacks is less than half that of whites. Unemployment among blacks is three times that of white Floridians, and the number of black families living in poverty is five times that of whites.

Nevertheless, life for many of the fourteen percent of Floridians who are African-American has improved in recent decades. Today, most Florida cities are less segregated than the typical American city. One in seven blacks employed in Florida works in a professional or managerial job. The gap between black and white infant mortality rates and black and white high school students' scores on standardized tests is slowly shrinking.

African Americans have also gradually made headway in Florida's business and political worlds. In 1992, three African-American Floridians were elected to the U.S. Congress, marking the first time since Reconstruction that blacks have represented Florida in Washington.

TAMPA AND MIAMI

Florida's most diverse cities are Tampa and Miami. Before the turn of the century, Ybor (pronounced EE-bore) City, later part of Tampa, became the center of the United States' cigar-manufacturing industry. Many of the cigar makers were Cuban Americans, and Southern and Eastern Europe provided the rest of the workforce. With so many immigrants from Cuba, Spain, and Italy, Tampa developed a mixed Mediterranean and Latin culture.

This culture was also largely Roman Catholic, which displeased some members of Florida's Protestant majority. In 1916, Democrat Sidney Catts won election as Florida's governor on an anti-Catholic platform. Over time, anti-Catholicism fell out of favor across the country. In 1986, voters elected the state's first Catholic governor, Bob Martinez, a former Tampa mayor of Spanish origin.

TEN LARGEST CITIES

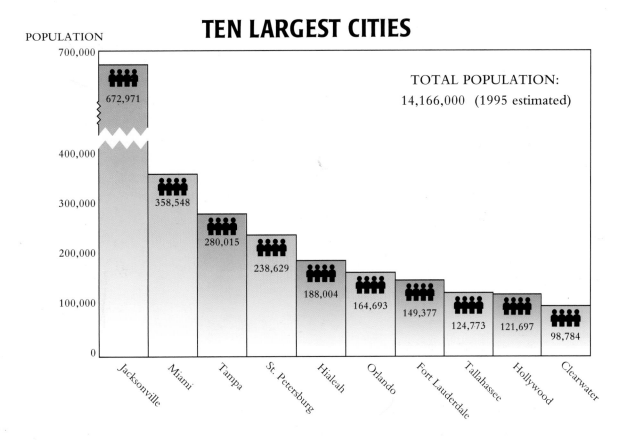

POPULATION

TOTAL POPULATION:
14,166,000 (1995 estimated)

700,000

672,971

400,000

358,548

300,000

280,015

238,629

200,000

188,004

164,693

149,377

124,773

121,697

100,000

98,784

0

Jacksonville Miami Tampa St. Petersburg Hialeah Orlando Fort Lauderdale Tallahassee Hollywood Clearwater

Florida's current multicultural center is Miami. In 1959, a revolutionary army led by Fidel Castro seized power in Cuba. Castro's political foes and many professionals and businesspeople fled the island nation. Many of these Cuban exiles eventually settled in Miami. To survive, these well-educated immigrants frequently had to take jobs as waiters and taxi drivers, but only temporarily. They soon started stores and restaurants, mainly in the Miami neighborhood that is now called Little Havana.

In 1980, more than a hundred thousand people left Cuba for Florida during what became known as the Mariel boatlift. Most of these

Many of the first Cubans to arrive in Florida were cigar makers, a trade that lives on today.

new immigrants were poor, and some were convicted criminals. Even Miami's established Cubans were ambivalent about the newcomers, particularly because the boatlift made some white Floridians more hostile to all Hispanics. Upset about the influx of immigrants, irate south Florida voters tried to ban the use of Spanish in government activities by passing an English-only ordinance.

This slap in the face energized Miami's Cuban community. Cuban exiles developed a Cuban-American economic and political presence in south Florida. "We knew how to speak the language of the

Venezuelans and the Brazilians and the Argentineans in world trade," says Enrique Viciana, a Cuban-American accountant. "Miami became a market for Spanish speakers, even from Europe."

Today, a separate, largely Cuban-American editorial staff produces a Spanish-language edition of the *Miami Herald* aimed at all of Latin America. Cuban Americans currently serve as mayors of Miami and Dade County, and two Cuban Americans represent south Florida in the U.S. House of Representatives.

In Miami's Little Havana district, a thriving Cuban-American community enjoys such treats as thick, dark Cuban coffee.

WHO OWNS THE PAST?

Florida's various ethnic groups sometimes argue over how the state's troubled history should be presented. Although the Seminole Wars took place over a century ago, their heroes—on both sides—can still ignite passions today.

Every year since 1968, the Springtime Tallahassee Festival parade has been led by a man dressed like Andrew Jackson. Festival defenders maintain that this recognizes Jackson as an important and colorful figure in Florida's development. But almost every year critics complain that this glorifies Jackson, who they believe was viciously brutal to Native Americans and African Americans. "Blacks and Indians today can no more be expected to revere Andrew Jackson than Jews could be expected to revere Hitler," Tallahassee journalist Roosevelt Wilson wrote during the 1993 springtime brouhaha.

The mascot of Tallahassee's Florida State University is the Seminole. FSU fans developed the "tomahawk chop," an up-down arm motion that Atlanta Braves baseball fans later picked up. Before every FSU home football game, a man playing Osceola rides a horse into the center of the field and plants a burning spear. Florida's Seminole leaders have approved these practices, but Native American activists from other states have objected. "It's disgusting to the native people to see this trivializing of Indian culture," says Indian activist Clyde Bellecourt.

Although Cuban Americans now form south Florida's largest ethnic community, other groups also dot the cultural landscape. Northern Jewish retirees have been moving to south Florida beaches for several decades. Today, the region has the second-largest Jewish population of any U.S. metropolitan area. Haitians and Nicaraguans fleeing economic and political problems in their home countries have settled in Miami, too. They often work alongside other Caribbean and Central American migrants in south Florida's farms. Native Americans descended from the survivors of the Seminole Wars still live on nearby reservations. All these groups have faced discrimination, but most have slowly made a niche for themselves in south Florida's multicultural society.

CULTURAL DIVISIONS

Florida is not always a multicultural paradise. Conflicts between Miami's Cuban Americans and African Americans made headlines in the 1980s. African Americans resented the Cuban Americans' business and political success. They were also convinced that,

ETHNIC FLORIDA

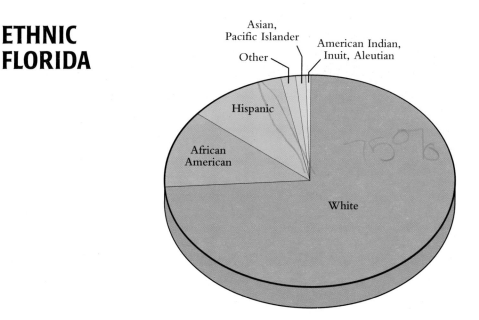

Although most Native Americans were driven out of Florida in the nineteenth century, 1,500 Seminole still live in the state.

while the government welcomed Cubans with open arms, blacks continued to experience police harassment and discrimination. This anger bubbled to the surface in a series of riots in Miami and other Florida cities throughout the 1980s.

There are also regional conflicts within Florida. Many northern Floridians have never been to Miami, and vice versa. Common phrases illustrate this division. Journalist Eugene Patron says Miami residents joke that traveling north into Fort Lauderdale is like "going back to America." Broward County historian Helen Landers says a popular bumper sticker reads: "Would the last American that leaves Miami bring the American flag?"

But Florida's diverse cultural communities often mingle and get along. Clarke Campbell-Evans is pastor at a Methodist church in North Miami, where the congregation is a veritable United Nations. Members of his church come from thirty different countries. Walking through the neighborhood, Campbell-Evans commonly hears people speaking at least four different languages—Portuguese, Spanish, English, and Creole (a version of French spoken by Haitians). Despite the persistence of cultural conflicts, he says he loves the "cosmopolitan mix" that is typical of south Florida.

THE MELTING POT

Even Floridians who don't always appreciate the state's cultural diversity concede that it has produced a wonderful array of foods, ranging from Southern to Cuban to Mexican to Jewish.

Among Florida's specialties are grilled alligator, key lime pie, fried chicken, hush puppies, collard greens, cheese grits, fried catfish, stuffed flounder, watermelon, country fried steak, hog jowls (pig cheeks), cheese blintzes, burritos, black bean soup, Cuban bread, plantains, and iced tea (with lemon, sugar, and mint). "I don't think Florida has a huge, distinct cuisine like New Orleans," says north Florida journalist Gary Fineout. "I think it's a blend."

As popular as eating and sizing up the neighbors may be, Floridians probably spend more of their leisure time enjoying the warm weather outdoors or trying to escape it in shopping malls and sports bars.

FUN AND GAMES

In most of Florida, football is king. Come Friday night, Floridians are generally in the stadium or glued to their television sets. Watching football is all the more tempting because Florida teams—high school, college, and professional—are so good. In recent years, Florida's college teams have often vied for the nation's number one ranking.

One activity that will lure Floridians into watching sports other than football is gambling. Floridians bet legally on south Florida horse racing and north Florida dog racing. But the state's most distinctive gambling sport is *jai alai* (pronounced HIGH-LIE). Spaniards invented this game, and in Florida Cuban-American players dominate it. It resembles a fast-paced combination of racquetball and badminton.

Many Floridians too old to play contact sports aren't necessarily content to sit in stadiums or in front of the television and watch. Golf courses and tennis courts blanket south Florida's coasts.

RECIPE: THE CUBAN SANDWICH

Floridians have enjoyed much Cuban-influenced food in recent decades. But the best-known Cuban-American dish is not actually from Cuba. In fact, turn-of-the-century Cuban-American cooks invented the "Cuban sandwich" in Tampa. Nevertheless, today the dish is popular throughout the state, from Miami's Little Havana all the way to north Florida. Have an adult help you with this recipe:

fresh Cuban bread
Swiss cheese
raw onions (optional)
lettuce (optional)
mustard
sliced ham
sliced roast pork
pickles

Authentic Cuban bread is flat and circular, shaped somewhat like a flying saucer. If you can't find Cuban bread, French, Italian, or any light, fluffy bread will do.

Slice the bread in two the long way. Slice the cheese and shred the lettuce and onions, if you're using them. Spread mustard on the bread and insert the meat, cheese, pickles, lettuce, and onions.

To complete the sandwich, you need to grill and press it. Because Cuban presses are hard to come by, you might use the flat, ungrooved side of a waffle iron, two iron skillets (one on each side of the sandwich), or even an iron. Once the sandwich has been flattened, enjoy.

Jai alai is sometimes called the world's fastest game, because balls often reach speeds up to 175 miles per hour.

Florida's endless beaches provide plenty of opportunity to surf.

Because of Florida's warm weather, golfers and tennis players can play throughout the year, although thunderstorms can end games suddenly.

SUN AND SURF

Florida is a mecca for water enthusiasts. Coral reefs and shipwrecks near the Florida Keys and sinkholes, springs, and underwater caves in north Florida draw scuba divers. Northeast and central Florida's Atlantic coast beaches attract surfers.

Florida scuba divers and surfers talk in similar hushed tones about their tranquil experiences out in the ocean. "It's a different world down there," says Jay Stemmen about scuba diving in the gulf. "It's peaceful. Nobody talks. You're just enjoying the water and the environment." "I've never been closer to God than one day out there," Kurt Eichin says about surfing at his favorite Space Coast beach. "All by myself, huge waves. There was completely gray skies. I couldn't tell which way was east or west by the sun. I was the only one out there. I couldn't see any people or cars."

But surfers and scuba divers face a common danger in the waters off Florida: sharks. Scuba diver Kevin Sweeney likes to spearfish near Florida's coral reefs. If hungry sharks appear when Sweeney has a bag full of bloody fish, he says he knows exactly what to do with the bag: "Give it to 'em. Drop it, and get out of there."

Many Floridians enjoy the great outdoors closer to home by maintaining attractive lawns and swimming pools. This isn't always fun, however. Because Florida's climate is warm and rainy for so much of the year, mowing the lawn can be an endless task. "You

Sharks live in the waters off Florida, giving scuba divers and fishermen reason for caution.

Fishing is popular among young and old alike in Florida.

can watch it grow when it's raining," says north Florida's Mike Santarone.

Before they're old enough to play football, surf, or mow the lawn, Florida kids learn how to swim. Swimming lessons at an early age are so common that kids who haven't learned by age eight or nine are often too embarrassed to admit it. Boys, in particular, also often enjoy the outdoors by fishing.

Florida's warm weather pushes Floridians of every background toward the swimming pool, the beach, and the football stadium. These common pleasures help unite the state's residents, despite their tremendous diversity.

5 RESHAPING THE NATION

Universal Studios

Many people from around the world, some famous and some not so famous, have helped set Florida's course today. But Florida's own sons and daughters have also shaped the direction of the nation.

TWO WRITERS

Between the world wars, folklorist and novelist Zora Neale Hurston made a name for herself as one of the first writers to celebrate the rural black experience. Hurston grew up in Eatonville, an all-black agricultural town north of Orlando, and then moved to New York City to study anthropology at Barnard College. While in New York, she became associated with prominent figures in the Harlem Renaissance, a cultural movement of African-American writers, musicians, and poets. But Hurston found herself drawn regularly back to her home state.

There she gathered the material for such books as *Mules and Men*, a study of folk culture, and *Their Eyes Were Watching God*, a novel about a powerful, independent black woman. Hurston's vigorous humor and compelling stories earned her many admirers. She showed blacks as real flesh-and-blood characters, with their share of flaws. Her books were far ahead of their time in that they took the culture of poor rural blacks seriously.

For Zora Neale Hurston, Florida was a place "where personal strength and courage were the highest virtues. People were supposed to take care of themselves without whining."

Although these themes were common in the 1930s and early 1940s, by the 1950s, they had fallen out of favor. Hurston continued her work quietly in Florida, but without drawing any attention. Before her death in 1960, she even had to work as a maid to support herself. But in the 1970s and 1980s, interest in feminism and black literature revived. Hurston's work was rediscovered, bringing her a level of acclaim and popularity that she had never enjoyed during her lifetime.

Marjorie Kinnan Rawlings was another writer who chronicled the lives of Florida's rural poor, both black and white. Rawlings, a white woman originally from the North, lived and worked at Cross

The beauty of north Florida captivated northerner Marjorie Kinnan Rawlings, who settled in Cross Creek and wrote about the area.

Creek, near Gainesville. In 1938, she wrote *The Yearling*, an award-winning novel about a twelve-year-old farm boy and his pet fawn.

A NEW DEALER

One of the greatest supporters of President Franklin Roosevelt's New Deal policies in the 1930s was Florida's Claude Pepper. After taking office in 1933 in the depths of the Great Depression,

Roosevelt tried to provide all Americans with jobs and security in the form of government work programs, old-age pensions, unemployment compensation, and benefits for disabled people and families with children. He called this the New Deal.

Running as a staunch New Dealer, young Claude Pepper, a north Florida lawyer, won a seat in the U.S. Senate in 1936. Pepper went on to cast key votes for New Deal measures such as the minimum wage and the forty-hour work week.

Pepper eventually lost his Senate seat, but he was elected to the House of Representatives in time to defend the Social Security system, one of the New Deal's most cherished programs. A champion of the elderly, he served in the House until his death in 1989 at age eighty-eight.

CIVIL RIGHTS LEADERSHIP

Another Floridian important to President Roosevelt was north Florida educator Mary McLeod Bethune. In 1904, Bethune founded the school that became Bethune-Cookman College, one of Florida's four predominantly black colleges. Bethune was both a friend of First Lady Eleanor Roosevelt and an official in the Roosevelt Administration. For nine years, she was Roosevelt's special advisor on minority affairs. In 1936, she became the first black woman to head a federal agency when she was appointed director of the Division of Negro Affairs of the National Youth administration. Bethune fought for civil rights throughout her career and helped found the National Council of Negro Women.

Another important early civil rights advocate from Florida was

Mary McLeod Bethune was endlessly energetic and determined. "Go ahead and do it," she told a friend who said a job couldn't be done.

James Weldon Johnson. Johnson had been a schoolteacher in his hometown of Jacksonville but left for New York City after local whites nearly lynched him for socializing with a light-skinned woman they thought was white. In 1920, Johnson became the first African-American executive secretary of the National Association for the Advancement of Colored People. In this role, Johnson fought hard for passage of a federal antilynching law but was unsuccessful.

A true renaissance man, Johnson made his mark in many different fields. He was a lawyer as well as an accomplished poet and essayist.

James Weldon Johnson's most famous song, "Lift Every Voice and Sing," begins, "Lift every voice and sing/Till earth and heaven ring/Ring with the harmonies of liberty."

He served as the United States consul to Venezuela and Nicaragua. He and his brother, John Rosamond Johnson, wrote two hundred songs for Broadway shows. They also penned "Lift Every Voice and Sing," which is often called the black national anthem.

Today, Johnson is probably best remembered for his classic novel *The Autobiography of an Ex-Colored Man.* Published in 1912, this was the first novel by an African American written in the voice of the main character, expressing fully his thoughts, feelings, and vision of the world. It tells the story of a black man whose skin is so light he can pass for white. To escape racial violence and discrimination, he eventually moves north and lives his life out as a white man. Near the novel's end, the narrator compares his life to the work of the African-American leaders of the day: "Beside them I feel small and selfish. I am an ordinary successful white man who has made a little money. They are men who are making history and a race. I, too, might have taken part in a work so glorious."

During the early days of the civil rights movement, Florida governor LeRoy Collins became a national champion of Southern moderation. He walked the fine line of supporting racial equality without alienating white voters. As governor, he played a crucial role in preventing the Florida legislature from making laws defending segregation. Collins eventually served as President Lyndon Johnson's emissary to the civil rights movement.

MAKING MUSIC

Florida musicians have helped bridge cultural gaps that have stumped politicians both in the civil rights era and today. In the 1950s, the South gave birth to rock 'n' roll, which has its roots in black music. But for a long time, country remained the music of choice among white Floridians.

Still, it was two young white musicians from Daytona who helped expose Floridians to the music of the great African-American blues veterans. In the late 1960s, Duane and Gregg Allman formed a band that played the Jacksonville area regularly. The band drew inspiration from blues music, sometimes covering songs by such legends as John Lee Hooker. Many young white Floridians started listening to the blues after hearing about it from the Allman brothers.

SPEAKING OUT FOR CIVIL RIGHTS

In 1960, Florida governor LeRoy Collins delivered a talk on race relations at a Jacksonville radio station. Because Collins took on civil rights opponents more directly than usual, this unscripted talk gained attention across the state and the nation. After stating that America's "racial strife" helped enemies of the United States around the world, Collins continued:

> I made that statement the other day and somebody said to me, "Yes, I think you are right about that. We understand how that injures our nation for the word to be passed along about our racial strife, but all this could be eliminated if the colored people would just stay in their place."
>
> Now friends, that's not a Christian point of view. That's not a democratic point of view. That's not a realistic point of view. We can never stop Americans from struggling to be free. We can never stop Americans from hoping and praying that some day in some way this ideal that is imbedded in our Declaration of Independence . . . that all men are created equal, that that somehow will be a reality and not just an illusory distant goal.

The Allman Brothers Band lasted in its original form just long enough to produce an album considered one of rock's best, *Live at the Fillmore East*. Separate motorcycle accidents claimed the lives of Duane Allman and another band member, Berry Oakley, within a thirteen-month period in the early 1970s. The musical genre that the Allman Brothers Band helped create became known as Southern rock. In its original form, Southern rock linked the music of white and black Southerners in a way that was previously unknown.

In the mid-1980s, a Florida band was stretching the boundaries of a different musical genre. Rap music got a lot of attention, not all of it good, when the south Florida band 2 Live Crew hit the charts. Lead vocalist Luther Campbell's rap style, with its violent and notoriously lewd lyrics, was a forerunner of what in the 1990s became known as gangsta rap. Campbell made headlines throughout the country when he was arrested during a concert in south Florida and charged with obscenity. Many people leaped to his defense, arguing that his right to free speech had been violated. Once the uproar had passed, 2 Live Crew faded away, to be replaced by rappers with more political lyrics. Today, Luther Campbell is a successful businessman in south Florida.

While 2 Live Crew was pointing rap in new directions, other south Florida musicians were connecting audiences to a new flavor of Latin-tinged dance music. The Miami Sound Machine's 1985 hit "Conga" had people across the country tapping their toes and hitting the dance floors. Two Miami Sound Machine vocalists, Cuban-Americans Gloria Estefan and Jon Secada, went on to become solo artists. Estefan, the more successful of the two, has recorded songs in both English and her native Spanish.

Pushing boundaries, gaining new audiences, creating new sounds, Florida's popular musicians have made the most of Florida's position as a cultural crossroads. Only time will tell what concoctions they will cook up in the future.

With a long string of hits in both English and Spanish, Gloria Estefan is one of the nation's most popular Hispanic entertainers.

The rap group 2 Live Crew hit the front page when lead vocalist Luther Campbell was arrested for obscenity.

6 TOURING THE PENINSULA

Spread across Florida's landscape is evidence of the state's diverse heritage. From the backwaters of northwest Florida to the coral reefs of the Florida Keys, the state is alive with nature, chock full of forts, and teeming with sights that lure tourists from all over the world.

THE BIG BEND

All around the Big Bend in Florida's panhandle is evidence of the state's Native American and African-American past. Florida's largest Native American mound site, the Lake Jackson Mounds, is northwest of Tallahassee. These large earthen mounds, which were apparently used for ceremonial and burial purposes, were built by Indians living in the area as long ago as A.D. 1000. Ironically, the three grassy mounds sit next to a lake named for Andrew Jackson, who helped drive Native Americans from Florida.

Southwest of Tallahassee is Fort Gadsden State Park, site of the Negro Fort, where many African Americans and Native Americans were killed by Jackson's troops. The site offers a great view of the slow-moving Apalachicola River. You'll need to bring bug spray almost any time of year.

The Big Bend also features some of the state's most beautiful, pristine, and uncrowded beaches, such as St. George Island, St.

Joseph Peninsula, and St. Andrews. The boat rides at Wakulla Springs, reportedly the world's deepest and largest freshwater spring, offer a great look at the lush environment of inland north Florida. Beware of the alligators.

NORTHEAST FLORIDA

In St. Augustine, on the Atlantic coast, the historic Spanish Castillo de San Marcos still stands. Across the street is the old Spanish

St. Joseph State Park on the Florida panhandle boasts one of the state's most pristine and undeveloped beaches.

Construction of the massive Castillo de San Marcos began in 1672 and took twenty-three years to complete.

Quarter, where craftspeople work in buildings from the eighteenth century. Further toward the center of town stand two opulent hotels built by Henry Flagler. One now houses a college, the other a museum that includes a magnificent collection of glasswork.

The beaches between St. Augustine and Daytona Beach are among the few in the country that licensed motorists can drive on. The beaches are wide and made of hard, packed sand, which make them a great place to drive. Speed zones, entrance fees, and one-way routes limit the fun. The practice is controversial, for both environmental and safety reasons.

Early February brings Bike Week, when motorcyclists from around the country descend on Daytona Beach. Later in the month stock car racing enthusiasts crowd the city for the Daytona 500.

Inland, in northwest Gainesville, is Devil's Millhopper, a deep, dry sinkhole. A long staircase enables visitors to descend far into the hole.

TAMPA BAY AND SOUTHWEST FLORIDA

Tampa showcases its multicultural heritage in the Ybor City district. A small museum illustrates the history of the area's cigar-making economy and immigrant culture. The other Ybor City highlight is the Columbia restaurant, perhaps the state's best-known eating establishment, which has been operating for more than ninety years. In a covered courtyard, visitors enjoy dining on the restaurant's specialty, *paella* (pronounced pie-AY-yah), a mixture of yellow rice, chicken, and seafood.

Across the Hillsborough River lies Henry Plant's old Tampa Bay Hotel, complete with minarets. The hotel is now part of the University of Tampa. A more recent tourist destination is Busch Gardens. No Anheuser-Busch factory makes beer here anymore. Instead, monorails carry visitors around a park filled with African wildlife.

Tampa comes alive during early February with two big events. The Gasparilla Pirate Fest begins with a mock invasion of the city by men masquerading as the legendary José Gaspar and his band of pirates. They sail into Tampa, land, and parade through downtown. The following week, northeastern Tampa is the site of the Florida State Fair, a two-week extravaganza complete with rides, rodeos, livestock and horse shows, and nightly concerts.

When the Tampa Bay Hotel was built in 1891 for an astonishing $3 million, it was the ultimate in luxury. The rooms were lavishly furnished with art and antiques from all over the world and a train delivered guests right to the entrance.

Across wide Tampa Bay is St. Petersburg, a newer, largely Midwestern retirement community. The highlight of St. Petersburg's waterfront is the Salvador Dali Museum. The museum features the world's largest collection of the Spanish surrealist's bizarre paintings and sculpture, including some gargantuan oil masterpieces.

South of Tampa Bay is Sarasota, long the headquarters of the Ringling Brothers and Barnum & Bailey Circus—the Greatest Show on Earth. Circus tycoon John Ringling made his home there. A complex of buildings off Sarasota Bay pays homage to the Ringling family and the circus. The complex includes a wonderful circus memorabilia museum, an art museum with European paintings collected by the Ringling family, and the Ringling mansion.

Farther south, on the Gulf coast near Fort Myers, are Sanibel and Captiva Islands, which have some of the best seashell-hunting ground in the state. Watch out for your bare feet.

ORLANDO AND THE SPACE COAST

Orlando is Florida's biggest tourist area. Disney World officials are in the process of adding new attractions and revamping the Magic

Shells blanket some of Florida's west coast beaches.

Kingdom. Increasingly, the park features not only old Disney cartoon characters like Mickey Mouse and Donald Duck but also characters from Disney's newer animated musicals, such as The *Little Mermaid*'s Ariel and *The Lion King's* Simba. New attractions include MGM-Disney Studios and Animal Kingdom.

Some Floridians never tire of Disney. Mary Eichin, who grew up near Orlando, says she has been to Disney World roughly thirty times, even once sneaking in without paying. "I felt very guilty," says Eichin.

Another fun Orlando site is Universal Studios, where the rides and attractions are all based on the movies. You can hop on a bicycle for a ride through the air with E.T., learn how the movies make fake earthquakes, or watch make-up artists create gory monsters.

The only central Florida attraction that rivals Disney in size and originality is the Kennedy Space Center. New, high-tech programs and IMAX shows bring the far reaches of space that much closer. But a simple bus ride past the launchpads and the gigantic Vehicle Assembly Building, where technicians put together the Apollo rockets, can be equally satisfying.

SOUTH-CENTRAL FLORIDA

Less well known but just as interesting is the interior of the southern half of the peninsula. There, farmworkers, wayward tourists,

Frankenstein's monster signs an autograph at Universal Studios.

A visit to the Kennedy Space Center provides a close-up view of rockets.

poorer retirees, and Native Americans share a less densely populated area of orange groves, sugarcane fields, phosphate strip
mines, and wide prairies.

Although most of the state's orange groves are now farther south,
the Florida Citrus Tower still rises above Clermont. Visitors can

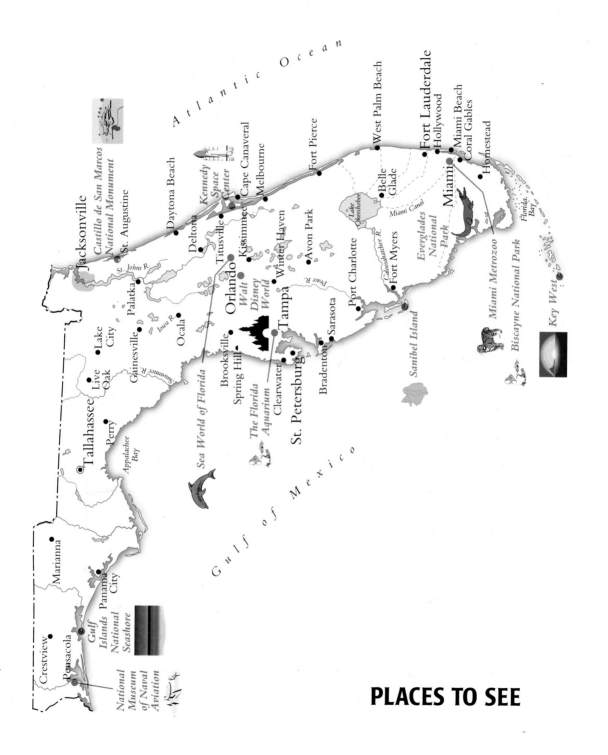

Atlantic Ocean

West Palm Beach
Fort Lauderdale
Hollywood
Miami Beach
Coral Gables
Homestead

Belle
Glade
Miami Canal

Castillo de San Marcos
National Monument
St. Augustine

Jacksonville

Daytona Beach

Deltona

Kennedy
Space
Center
Cape Canaveral
Melbourne

Fort Pierce

Lake
Okeechobee

Miami

St. Johns R.

Titusville
Kissimmee
Winter Haven
Avon Park

Everglades
National
Park

Caloosahatchee R.

Florida
Bay

Orlando
Walt
Disney
World

Palatka

Iowa R.

Ocala

Gainesville

Live
Oak

Lake
City

Brooksville
Spring Hill

Tampa

Sarasota
Bradenton

Port Charlotte
Peace R.

Fort Myers

Sanibel Island

Miami Metrozoo

Biscayne National Park

Key West

Sea World of Florida

The Florida
Aquarium
Clearwater
St. Petersburg

Suwannee R.

Tallahassee

Perry

Appalachee
Bay

Gulf of Mexico

Crestview

Marianna

Pensacola
Gulf
Islands
National
Seashore
Panama
City

National Museum
of Naval Aviation

PLACES TO SEE

ride an elevator up the tower for the magnificent view. In tiny Mulberry, south of Lakeland, the curious Florida Phosphate Museum illustrates changes in the state's only major mining industry. Back off the highway between Orlando and Titusville, the Fort Christmas Museum chronicles the Second Seminole War, as well as the life of central Florida's poor rural families and the rise of the area's cattle-ranching industry.

South of Lake Okeechobee stretch the northern Everglades. Easily the most interesting stop in the area is Shark Valley. Like most outdoor south Florida locales, this is an attraction that people should visit only in the winter months. During the summer, the heat and mosquitoes are much too oppressive. At Shark Valley, a paved trail leads south from the cross-Everglades Tamiami Trail deep into the Everglades and back. Less agile or adventurous visitors can take a tram along the trail, which ends at a tall observation deck. Others may want to rent bicycles to ride to and from the observation tower.

Besides the stupendous view of the Everglades from the tower, Shark Valley's big draw is its alligators. Hundreds of gators crowd the ponds around the observation tower. On the trail, mother and baby alligators may sprint in front of your bike.

MIAMI AND THE GOLD COAST

Both the Tamiami Trail and Interstate 75, dubbed Alligator Alley, head east into Florida's largest metropolitan area, Miami–Fort Lauderdale–West Palm Beach. Extending west out of downtown Miami is *Calle Ocho*, "Eighth Street" in Spanish. The street is the

The Everglades' Shark Valley is teeming with alligators.

center of Little Havana, where a McDonald's with Spanish-language signs is just one of the symbols of the Latin American presence in Miami.

Another symbol of Miami's Cuban-American population is the old *Miami News* building, dubbed Freedom Tower. In the 1960s and 1970s, U.S. authorities turned this building into Miami's version of Ellis Island. There they processed thousands of Cuban exiles entering the country.

Across Biscayne Bay is Miami Beach. There South Beach's sultry

FLORIDA FOLK FESTIVAL AND CALLE OCHO

They take place on opposite ends of the Florida peninsula, on opposite ends of spring. Even though both are multicultural celebrations of Florida's diversity, they seem like opposite extremes. One takes place amid the bright lights and noisy hubbub of a tropical city lined with skyscrapers. The other sits in the shade of oaks and Spanish moss along a slow, winding river on the outskirts of a sleepy Old South town. They are Florida's two most noteworthy annual festivals: the Florida Folk Festival and Calle Ocho, part of the larger Carnaval Miami.

Each March, the Miami event showcases south Florida's Latin heritage. It started in 1978 as a fifteen-block open-house party on Eighth Street, Calle Ocho, in the heart of Miami's Little Havana. That year, the event drew a hundred thousand people. Ten years later, it drew a million. Advertised as the world's largest block party, the festival features the food, music, dance, and folk art of countries from around the Americas.

Seven hours north of Miami is White Springs, the tiny resort town that hosts the Florida Folk Festival. Billed as the nation's oldest official state folk festival, the three-day event showcases storytelling and fiddling from Florida's rural white culture and also features traditions from African-American, Native American, and Latin American cultures. During one weekend each May, twenty thousand people stroll the festival's lush grounds, enjoying dance, music, and arts and crafts demonstrations.

nightclubs and pastel art deco buildings line Ocean Drive. Art deco was a style popular in the 1920s and 1930s that used bold, streamlined designs. Miami architects put their own local spin on the style, depicting palm trees and flamingos in the buildings' intricate designs. South Beach's eight hundred art deco buildings make up the largest collection of it anywhere. Walking through the chic neighborhood, admiring the exuberant buildings, you also might see models and movie stars, because South Beach is a popular spot among the fashion set.

South Beach is renowned for its colorful art deco architecture.

Visitors to Key Largo explore the undersea world.

THE EVERGLADES AND THE KEYS

The roads leading southwest out of Miami travel directly through the winter vegetable fields into Everglades National Park. In the winter, the park is a bird lover's paradise, as migratory fowl from all over North America spend the season there. At Flamingo, the southernmost place in the continental United States, at the very tip of the park, camping and canoe rentals are available.

It's also possible to camp across the bay on Key Largo, the first major key. Key Largo sits on the edge of one of Florida's major coral reefs. From John Pennekamp Coral Reef State Park, visitors can see the reef by snorkeling or taking glass-bottomed boats. Visitors prone to seasickness should think twice about taking the boats. The authorities are actually trying to curb boat traffic around the reefs, so you can tell your friends you're not queasy—you're just trying to save the environment.

THE FLAG: The Florida state flag, adopted in 1899, has the state seal on a field of white. Four red bars extend out from the seal to the corners of the flag.

THE SEAL: The state seal shows the sun's rays shining over a coastal scene, which includes a Seminole woman spreading flowers, a Sabal palmetto tree, and a steamboat on the water. Above the scene are the words "Great Seal of the State of Florida." Below the scene is the state motto, "In God We Trust." In use since 1868, the seal was adopted in 1985 after changes were made to the original.

STATE SURVEY

Statehood: March 3, 1845

Origin of Name: Florida was named by Spanish explorer Juan Ponce de León in April 1513. He may have chosen the name because he arrived in the area during the Easter celebration, known as *Pascua Florida*, or "Feast of the Flowers" in Spanish. Or he may have named the land Florida because of the many flowers he found there.

Nickname: Sunshine State

Capital: Tallahassee

Motto: In God We Trust

Flower: Orange blossom

Tree: Sabal palmetto palm

Bird: Mockingbird

Fish: Largemouth bass (freshwater); Atlantic sailfish (saltwater)

Insect: Praying mantis

Animal: Florida panther

Mammal: Manatee (freshwater); dolphin (saltwater)

Orange blossom

Mockingbird

OLD FOLKS AT HOME

(Swannee River)

Stephen Foster wrote "Old Folks at Home" in 1851. He was living in New York at the time and had never visited the South when he wrote the song. His nostalgic view of the Old South strikes us today as somewhat out of date. "Old Folks at Home" became Florida's official state song in 1935, but currently there is a growing movement to find a more up-to-date song to represent the state.

By Stephen Collins Foster

All roun' the little farm I wandered,
When I was young;
Then many happy days I squandered,
Many the songs I sung.
When I was playing with my brother,
Happy was I;
Oh! Take me to my kind old mother,
There let me live and die.
Chorus

One little hut among the bushes,
One that I love,
Still sadly to my mem'ry rushes,
No matter where I rove.
When will I see the bees a-humming
All roun' the comb?
When will I hear the banjo strumming,
Down in my good old home?
Chorus

Reptile: Alligator

Stone: Agatized coral

Gem: Moonstone

Shell: Florida horse conch

Soil: Mayakka fine sand

GEOGRAPHY

Highest Point: 345 feet above sea level near Lakewood in Walton County

Lowest Point: sea level along the coasts

Area: 58,560 square miles

Greatest Distance, North to South: 450 miles

Greatest Distance, East to West: 465 miles

Bordering States: Alabama to the north and west; Georgia to the north

Hottest Recorded Temperature: 109°F at Monticello on June 29, 1931

Coldest Recorded Temperature: -2°F at Tallahassee on February 13, 1899

Average Annual Precipitation: 54 inches

Major Rivers: Apalachicola, Aucilla, Blackwater, Caloosahatchee, Choctawhatchee, Escambia, Hillsborough, Kissimmee, Ochlockonee, Peace, Perdido, St. Johns, St. Marys, Suwannee, Withlacoochee

Major Lakes: Apopka, Blue Cypress, Crescent, George, Harney, Harris,

Iamonia, Istokpoga, Kissimmee, Monroe, Okeechobee, Orange, Talquin, Tohopekaliga

Trees: Bahama lysiloma, balk cypress, black tupelo, custard-apple, Florida fiddlewood, gumbo-limbo, laurel oak, live oak, longleaf pine, red mangrove, red maple, Sabal palmetto palm, slash pine, southern bayberry, southern red cedar, strangler fig, sweet bay, water hickory

Wild Plants: azalea, bougainvillea, bromeliad, cactus, camellia, coreopsis, dogwood, gardenia, golden begonia, hibiscus, iris, lupine, magnolia, mallow, marsh pink, oleander, orchid, pitcher plant, red bud, spider lily, sunflower, wood lily

Animals: black bear, dolphin, Florida panther, gray fox, Key deer, manatee, mangrove fox squirrel, marsh rabbit, opossum

Birds: anhinga, bald eagle, black-bellied tree duck, bobwhite quail, great blue heron, great egret, ibis, mangrove cuckoo, osprey, pelican, pileated woodpecker, reddish egret, redheaded woodpecker, red-winged blackbird, robin, roseate spoonbill, white-crowned pigeon, wild turkey, wood stork

Great blue heron

Fish: bluefish, bluegill, catfish, chub, crappie, Chipola bass, Florida largemouth bass, grouper, killfish, mackerel, marlin, menhaden, pompano, red snapper, sailfish, sea trout, striped bass, Suwannee bass, tarpon

Endangered Animals: American crocodile, Anastasia Island beach mouse, Atlantic green turtle, Atlantic hawksbill turtle, Atlantic Ridley turtle,

Bachman's warbler, Cape Sable seaside sparrow, Choctawhatchee beach mouse, Duke's saltmarsh vole, Everglades snail kite, Florida grass-hopper sparrow, Florida manatee, Florida mastiff bat, Florida panther, gray bat, humpback whale, ivory-billed woodpecker, Key deer, Key Largo cotton mouse, Key Largo woodrat, Kirtland's warbler, leatherback turtle, Lower Keys marsh rabbit, Okaloosa darter, Perdido Key beach mouse, Schaus' swallowtail butterfly, shortnose sturgeon, silver rice rat, sperm whale, wood stork

American crocodile

Endangered Plants: beautiful pawpaw, Brooksville bellflower, Chapman rhododendron, Cooley's water-willow, Florida golden aster, Florida bonamia, Florida torreya, Florida ziziphus, four-petal pawpaw, fragrant prickly-apple, Harper's beauty, Highlands scrub hypericum, Key tree-cactus, Miccosukee gooseberry, pygmy fringe tree, Rugel's pawpaw, scrub blazing star, scrub lupine, scrub mint, scrub plum, snakeroot, tiny polygala, wireweed

TIMELINE

Florida History

Early 1500s The Calusa, Tequesta, Jeaga, Ais, Timucua, Apalachee, Tocobaga, and Alachua live in present-day Florida

1513 Spanish explorer Juan Ponce de León claims Florida for Spain

1565 Pedro Menéndez de Avilés of Spain founds St. Augustine, the first permanent European settlement in what would become the United States

1704 English forces attack Florida, destroying Spanish missions in the north and burning most of St. Augustine

1750 Creek Indians leave Georgia and settle in Florida, where they are joined by ex-slaves and members of other Florida tribes and become known as the Seminoles

1763 Spain gives Florida to Great Britain in exchange for Cuba, which had been captured by the British in the Seven Years' War

1783 At the end of the American Revolution, Great Britain returns Florida to Spain

1817 The First Seminole War begins when Seminoles attack a boat carrying American soldiers on the Apalachicola River

1818 Andrew Jackson invades Florida, capturing Native American villages and Spanish towns

1821 Florida becomes part of the United States when Spain gives up its claim to the area

1824 Tallahassee becomes the permanent capital of Florida

1837 Seminole leader Osceola is captured by the Americans

1842 The Second Seminole War ends; many Seminoles are sent west; others move deep into the Everglades

1845 Florida becomes the 27th state

1851 The East Florida Seminary to train teachers opens at Ocala; the University of Florida develops from this school

1858 The Third Seminole War ends; fewer than 200 Seminoles remain in Florida

1861–1865 About 15,000 Floridians serve in the Confederate army during the Civil War

1868 Florida adopts a new constitution that allows blacks to vote and is readmitted to the Union

1896 Henry Morrison Flagler's railroad reaches Miami from the north, opening up south Florida to development

1925 Around 2.5 million people pour into Florida during the state's largest land boom

1947 Everglades National Park opens

1950 The air force launches the first missile from its Missile Test Center at Cape Canaveral

1961 Alan Shepard takes off in a rocket launched from Cape Canaveral, becoming the first American in space

1964 Dr. Martin Luther King Jr. leads demonstrations for equal rights for African Americans in St. Augustine

1980 Around 125,000 Cuban refugees come to Florida during the Mariel boatlift

1986 The space shuttle *Challenger* explodes after takeoff at Cape Canaveral, killing all seven crew members

1992 Hurricane Andrew, one of the greatest natural disasters in U.S. history, strikes south Florida; damages are estimated at $30 billion

ECONOMY

Agricultural Products: avocados, carrots, cattle, celery, cucumbers, eggs, grapefruit, hay, hogs, lettuce, limes, oranges, peanuts, peppers, potatoes, poultry, soybeans, strawberries, sugarcane, sweet corn, tangerines, tobacco, tomatoes, watermelons

Manufactured Products: aviation and aerospace equipment, chemicals, communications equipment, electrical equipment, medical instruments, processed foods, wood products

Natural Resources: cement, clay, crushed stone, lime, lumber, peat, phosphate, staurolite, zircon

Business and Trade: communications, finance, printing and publishing, real estate, tourism, transportation, retail trade

Citrus industry

CALENDAR OF CELEBRATIONS

Indian River Native American Festival View Native American arts and crafts and sample Native American foods at this January festival in New Smyrna. Dance contests and traditional storytelling are also part of the fun.

Olustee Battle Festival and Re-enactment More than 2,000 costumed

Civil War re-enactment

actors take part in the mock fighting as they re-enact the battle that saved Florida from Union soldiers during the Civil War. Held at Lake City in February, the festival also includes a parade and arts and crafts.

Florida State Fair Tampa is home to this February celebration of Florida's best. You can see arts and crafts and Florida farm animals, enjoy the carnival rides, and eat great fair food.

Chasco Fiesta This March festival in New Port Richey celebrates the friendship between the Calusa Indians and Spanish colonists. It includes a Native American pageant with costumes and dancing, arts and crafts, and sporting events.

Florida Strawberry Festival Plant City celebrates its claim as the Winter Strawberry Capital with 11 days of fun in March. Some of country music's biggest stars perform, and you can enjoy plenty of strawberries and other good food.

Florida Heritage Festival This April festival in Bradenton celebrates the local area's history. The festival's highlight is the re-enactment of Hernando De Soto's 1539 landing at the mouth of the Manatee River.

Fiesta of the Five Flags This festival celebrates Florida's history under the flags of Spain, France, Great Britain, the Confederacy, and the United States. The landing of a Spanish explorer is re-created, and ceremonies mark the raising and lowering of the flags of the different countries. Sand sculpting and a treasure hunt are also part of this June festival in Pensacola.

Billy Bowlegs Festival Pirates invade the Destin/Fort Walton Beach area in this June festival. Five hundred ships crowd the harbor in honor of local pirate legend Billy Bowlegs.

Caribbean Calypso Carnival The sounds of steel drums fill the air at this St. Petersburg festival in July, which features Caribbean music, food, and even limbo dancing.

Possum Festival and Parade Not many Florida festivals feature main dishes of baked possum and possum hash, but this one does. This August festival in Wausau also serves up food other than possum, as well as live music and a parade.

Hispanic Heritage Festival This monthlong Miami festival celebrates Spanish and Latin American culture. Hispanic folklore, arts and crafts, music, and foods are all part of the fun during this October event.

Florida Seafood Festival The state's oldest and largest seafood festival is held in Apalachicola every November. Oysters, crabs, and shrimp are the specialties here. For fun, try the oyster-shucking and net-throwing contests or watch the crab races.

Fort Myers Beach Sand Sculpture Contest At this November festival in Fort Myers Beach, you can watch professionals build the best sand castles around and join in the fun yourself.

Winterfest Boat Parade Fort Lauderdale is home to this December event that features more than 100 decorated boats.

STATE STARS

Mary McLeod Bethune (1875–1955), originally from South Carolina, became famous for her educational efforts in Florida. In 1904, she opened the Daytona Normal and Industrial Institute for African-American girls. In 1923, the school joined with the Cookman Institute for black men to become Bethune-Cookman College, where she served as president for many years. Bethune also went to Washington, D.C., to advise President Franklin Roosevelt on minority affairs.

Ray Charles (1930–   ), who was raised in Greenville, lost his sight by age seven. He began studying music at the St. Augustine School for Deaf and Blind Children. He went on to become an extremely influential musician by mixing gospel, rhythm and blues, and jazz to come up with soul music. His many hits include "Georgia on My Mind," "Hit the Road, Jack," and "What'd I Say."

Ray Charles

Jacqueline Cochran (1910?–1980) of Pensacola was the first woman to be elected to the Aviation Hall of Fame. After learning to fly, she became famous as a racing pilot. She organized the Women's Airforce Service Pilots (WASPS) during World War II and in 1953 became the first woman to fly faster than the speed of sound.

Walt Disney (1901–1966) brought his creative genius to Florida when he developed the Walt Disney World theme park in Lake Buena Vista.

Disney was famous for his animated films featuring such characters as Mickey Mouse and Donald Duck. He also started the Disneyland theme park in Anaheim, California.

Hamilton Disston (1844–1896), a northern businessman, proved that Florida's wetlands could be drained and made into valuable agricultural land. In 1881, Disston bought 4 million acres of land in central Florida and dug canals to drain the area. The city of Kissimmee grew as a result.

Marjory Stoneman Douglas (1890–   ) has written a number of books about Florida, including *The Everglades: River of Grass*, which has become a classic. Most famous for her environmental work, Douglas has also fought for women's rights and racial justice.

Gloria Estefan (1957–   ) moved to Miami from Cuba when she was two years old. She began her musical career with the Miami Sound Machine, who had their first big hit, "Anything for You," in 1988. She went on to a successful solo career. Following a bus accident that left her seriously injured, Estefan has made an inspirational comeback.

Marjory Stoneman Douglas

Chris Evert (1954–   ), who was born in Fort Lauderdale, is considered one of the greatest women tennis players of all time. Evert was the first woman player to earn $1 million. She counts three Wimbledon and six U.S. Open titles among her many wins.

Chris Evert

Mel Fisher (1922–   ) spent 16 years looking for the underwater wreckage of a Spanish boat that had sunk in 1622. When he finally found it near Key West in 1985, he became the best-known treasure hunter in the world. The silver, gold, and gems he recovered are worth as much as $4 billion. Much of the treasure is on display in a Key West museum.

Jackie Gleason (1916–1987) was the star of two of the most popular shows on early television, *The Jackie Gleason Show* and *The Honeymooners*. Although born in Brooklyn, New York, Gleason filmed both of his shows in Miami.

John Gorrie (1803–1855), a doctor, was living in Apalachicola in 1844 . To help cool his malaria patients, he built the world's first refrigeration machine, which produced blocks of ice.

Ernest Hemingway (1899–1961), who did much of his writing in Key West, is considered one of America's greatest authors. While living in Key West, Hemingway wrote *The Green Hills of Africa*, *For Whom the Bell Tolls*, and *To Have and Have Not*.

Zora Neale Hurston (1903–1960), an important African-American writer, was born in Eatonville. Hurston's writing often dealt with the culture and folklore of poor blacks in the South. Her works include the novel *Their Eyes Were Watching God*, the nonfiction study *Mules and Men*, and her autobiography, *Dust Tracks on a Road*.

Ernest Hemingway

James Weldon Johnson (1871–1938) of Jacksonville helped found the National Association for the Advancement of Colored People (NAACP) and served as its secretary for a number of years. He wrote poetry, song lyrics, and novels, most notably *The Autobiography of an Ex-Colored Man*. Johnson was also a United States diplomat to Venezuela and Nicaragua.

Sidney Lanier (1842–1881) is considered the best Southern poet of the late 1800s thanks to his works such as "Corn" and "The Marshes of Glynn." Although from Georgia, Lanier spent much time in Florida because of his poor health, and he wrote *Florida: Its Scenery, Climate, and History*, an early guidebook to the state.

Lue Gim Gong (1858–1925) was born in China. He moved to Massachusetts and then to Florida, where he developed a cold-resistant orange that is still grown there.

Osceola (1803?–1838) was a great Seminole leader who opposed the removal of his people from Florida. Osceola led the Seminoles during the Second Seminole War until he was captured. He later died while being held prisoner.

Ruth Bryan Owen (1855–1954), the daughter of politician William Jennings Bryan, moved to Miami to take a teaching position. Owen ran for the U.S. House of Representatives in 1928 and won, becoming the first woman from the Deep South to serve in Congress. She later became the first female U.S. diplomat when she served as minister to Denmark.

John D. Pennekamp (1898–1978) was editor of the *Miami Herald*. His campaign to save the Everglades from overdevelopment led to the creation of Everglades National Park. John Pennekamp Coral Reef State Park, near Key Largo, is named in his honor.

A. Philip Randolph (1889–1979), who was born in Crescent City, helped organize the Brotherhood of Sleeping Car Porters Union for African-American workers. Randolph was also a civil rights leader, who led marches on Washington, D.C., in 1941 and 1963.

Marjorie Kinnan Rawlings (1896–1953) began writing when she moved to Cross Creek. Her 1939 Pulitzer Prize–winning novel, *The Yearling*, is set in rural north Florida. Her book *Cross Creek* was made into a movie in 1983.

Janet Reno

Janet Reno (1938–   ), a Miami native, was the first woman to serve as attorney general of the United States. Previously, she had been elected attorney general of Florida five times.

Wesley Snipes (1962–   ), one of America's leading African-American actors, was born in Orlando. He then spent several years in New York, but during his teens, he returned to Orlando, where he took up acting. Snipes has starred in such films as *Passenger 57*, *Jungle Fever*, and *Rising Sun*.

Mel Tillis (1932–   ), a country music great, grew up in Pahokee. Tillis's songs, such as "Ruby, Don't Take Your Love to Town," have been recorded by many artists, including Jimmy Dean, the Everly Brothers, and Tom Jones. His daughter, Pam Tillis, who is also a popular country music singer, was born in Plant City.

Tiger Woods (1975–   ), who calls Orlando home, is the golfing sensation of the 1990s. After turning professional at age 21, Woods won the Masters Tournament in his first try as a pro.

Tiger Woods

Vicente Martinez Ybor (1818–1896) was a Cuban immigrant who made his fortune in cigar making. Ybor set up his first cigar factory in Key West, then moved to the Tampa area. Ybor City, the Cuban community that grew up around the cigar factories, later became part of Tampa.

TOUR THE STATE

Bird Emergency Aid and Kare Sanctuary (BEAKS) (Big Talbot Island) At the sanctuary, you can see how thousands of injured wild birds are cared for. Birds on view include eagles, pelicans, owls, and ospreys.

Castillo de San Marcos National Monument (St. Augustine) This massive fort built of shell rock by the Spanish in the late 1600s has walls 8- to 12-feet thick and 33-feet high. Inside, exhibits trace the history of the fort and St. Augustine. You might even get to see one of the fort's old cannons fired.

Daytona International Speedway (Daytona Beach) Known as the World Center of Racing, the speedway hosts many races, such as the Daytona 500 stock car race. You can tour the racetrack, watch videos of early races, and look over stock cars and other racing artifacts.

Daytona International Speedway

Kennedy Space Center (Cocoa Beach) The visitor center at this site features a moon rock, space vehicles, and many displays tracing the history of America's space program. You can also take a bus tour that provides views of the launchpads where space shuttles take off.

Mulberry Phosphate Fossil Museum (Mulberry) At this museum, you can view some of the dinosaur remains found in the area known as Bone Valley. Other exhibits focus on the history of phosphate mining.

Walt Disney World (Lake Buena Vista) Central Florida is home to the most popular vacation spot in the world. Walt Disney World is made up of three major theme parks, The Magic Kingdom, Epcot, and Disney-MGM Studios, along with a number of water parks and other attractions.

Universal Studios Florida (Orlando) Ever wonder how they do the scary makeup in horror movies or the great stunts in action movies? This is the place to find out. Shows and exhibits demonstrate how movies are made. Rides such as Kongfrontation, Jaws, and the E.T. Adventure let you become a part of some of your favorite movies.

Charles Hosmer Morse Museum of American Art (Winter Park) This museum features more than 4,000 works of American art. Pottery and paintings are on view, as are many beautiful stained-glass windows by the famed designer Louis Tiffany.

International Museum of Cartoon Art (Boca Raton) Displays at this museum range from early American political cartoons by Benjamin Franklin to current favorites such as Bugs Bunny. Exhibits feature comic strips, comic books, greeting cards, book illustrations, and drawings from animated movies.

Butterfly World (Coconut Creek) Here you can watch thousands of butterflies fluttering in two-story screened enclosures, which resemble gardens and a rain forest. You can also visit a butterfly breeding laboratory and a display of rare butterflies and insects from around the world.

International Swimming Hall of Fame (Fort Lauderdale) The world's greatest swimmers, including Johnny Weissmuller, Esther Williams, and Mark Spitz, are showcased at this site. Olympic medals and trophies are on display and an art gallery and videos help tell the story of competitive swimming.

Metrozoo (Miami) At this zoo, animals roam free in areas that look like their natural habitats. The Asian River Life exhibit contains leopards, monitors, and pythons. Rare Bengal white tigers can be found in a display that resembles the ruins of an Asian temple. The zoo also has playgrounds, animal shows, and a petting zoo.

Biscayne National Park (Miami) Ninety-five percent of this unusual national park is underwater. The park showcases a great variety of sea life, ranging from manatees to brightly colored parrot fish. Glass-bottomed boat trips are the best way to see the park's beautiful coral formations and tropical fish.

Everglades National Park (Homestead) This park is home to 25 species of mammals, more than 300 species of birds, and 60 reptile species, including the alligator. The Everglades has hiking trails, some with boardwalks, and tram rides from which you can view the wildlife.

Mel Fisher Maritime Heritage Society Museum (Key West) More than $40 million worth of treasure from old Spanish ships is on display at this museum. Gold, silver, emeralds, diamonds, brass cannons, and historic artifacts can be viewed. One gold chain is 12 feet long and weighs more than 6 pounds.

Henry Ford/Thomas Edison Winter Homes (Fort Myers) Friends Ford and Edison spent their winters together at these mansions in Fort Myers. The Ford home displays antique cars. The Edison home contains the inventor's laboratory, where he worked on the lightbulb and phonograph while on "vacation." A collection of Edison's inventions, ranging from talking dolls to the world's first record, are also on display.

Bailey-Matthews Shell Museum (Sanibel Island) This is the only museum in the country devoted entirely to shells. The 2 million shells here represent only one-third of all the types of shells in the world. The museum also contains interactive displays and shell art.

J. N. "Ding" Darling National Wildlife Refuge (Sanibel Island) Home to two hundred types of birds, including roseate spoonbills and brown pelicans, this park is a bird-watcher's paradise. There are both walking and driving trails through the refuge.

The John and Mable Ringling Museum of Art (Sarasota) John Ringling of

Ringling Brothers' Circus fame collected great works of European art, which are exhibited at his Sarasota home. Just as interesting as the art is the Circus Museum, located in another building on the grounds, which displays parade wagons, costumes, posters, photos, and other circus items.

Museum of Science and Industry (Tampa) This popular museum contains exhibits on everything from hurricanes to butterflies to the human body. Visitors can experience hurricane-strength winds in the Gulf Coast Hurricane exhibit. Then they can hike three miles of Florida wilderness in the Back Woods exhibit. Much of the museum features hands-on displays, such as fossils you can touch.

Pioneer Florida Museum (Dade City) Explore what it was like for Florida's pioneers at this museum, which includes an old schoolhouse, church, home, and railroad station. The museum also displays early farm tools, carriages, and Native American items.

Stephen Foster State Folk Culture Center (White Springs) Stephen Foster made the Suwannee River famous in his song "Old Folks at Home." Today, you can learn more about Foster and his songs here on the banks of the Suwannee. You can also see exhibits on Florida folk arts such as basket weaving, blacksmithing, and woodworking.

National Museum of Naval Aviation (Pensacola) The history of naval flight is the focus of this museum, where you can see famous navy fighter planes, such as the F-14 Tomcat, as well as models of aircraft carriers and early blimps. There are even hands-on displays that let you take the controls of navy training equipment.

FUN FACTS

The world's first scheduled commercial airplane flight was made in Florida in 1914. The seaplane, piloted by Tony Jannus, flew between St. Petersburg and Tampa.

Jacksonville is the largest city in the United States in land area. The city covers some 840 square miles.

Scuba divers can spend a night underwater at Jules' Undersea Lodge near Key Largo. The two-room hotel, originally an undersea research laboratory, sits 30 feet below the ocean's surface and has large windows which allow guests to view the life under the sea.

Florida has a bat hotel that has remained vacant for almost 70 years. Clyde Perky built the tower in 1929 on Sugarloaf Key to attract bats to eat the mosquitoes that were bothering guests at his fishing lodge. Perky even put bat droppings inside to encourage local bats to move in, but none ever did.

Florida has lots of sinkholes, places where the limestone roof of an underground cavern collapses, making a hole in the ground. The state's largest opened up in 1981 at Winter Park. It measured 300 feet across and 100 feet deep. One house, six cars, parts of two streets, and a swimming pool were swallowed up.

Florida has more thunderstorms than any other state. Fort Myers is the leading city for storms, with around 100 days with lightning each year.

FIND OUT MORE

If you want to learn more about Florida, look for these titles at your local library or bookstore.

GENERAL STATE BOOKS

Fradin, Dennis B. *Florida*. Chicago: Children's Press, 1992.

Sirvaitis, Karen. *Florida*. Minneapolis: Lerner, 1994.

SPECIAL INTEREST BOOKS

Billings, Charlene W. *Christa McAuliffe: Pioneer Space Teacher*. Hillside, N.J.: Enslow, 1986.

Bland, Celia. *Osceola: Seminole Rebel*. New York: Chelsea House, 1994.

Blassingame, Wyatt. *Ponce De Leon*. New York: Chelsea House, 1991.

Douglas, Marjory Stoneman. *The Everglades: River of Grass* (1947), rev. ed. Sarasota: Pineapple Press, 1997.

Greene, Katherine, and Richard Greene. *The Man Behind the Magic: The Story of Walt Disney*. New York: Viking, 1991.

Rawlings, Marjorie Kinnan. *Cross Creek*. New York: Charles Scribner's Sons, 1942

_____. *The Yearling*. New York: Charles Scribner's Sons, 1938.

Steffof, Rebecca. *Gloria Estefan*. New York: Chelsea House, 1991.

Tolbert-Rouchaleau, Jane. *James Weldon Johnson*. New York: Chelsea House, 1988.

VIDEOTAPES

Alligators and How They Live, with Additional Feature: Snakes and How They Live, revised ed. Diamond Entertainment Corp., 1992.

The Challenger Explosion. MPI Home Video, 1989.

Dive to the Coral Reefs. Lancit Media Productions, 1989.

Lost Man's River: An Everglades Journey. Mystic Fire Video, 1990.

Mary McLeod Bethune. Schlesinger Video Productions, 1994.

Over Florida. Wehman Video, 1992.

Racing for the Moon: America's Glory Days in Space. MPI Home Video, 1988.

Seminole. Schlesinger Video Productions, 1993.

The Yearling. MGM/UA Home Video, 1973.

CD-ROMS

Americans in Space: The Complete Historic Tour of Americans in Space. Multicom Publishing, 1993.

Discovering Endangered Wildlife: A Multimedia Expedition in Fun and Learning. Lyriq International Corp., 1995.

Sharks! Discovery Communications, 1994.

Space: A Visual History of Manned Spaceflight. Queue, Inc., 1993.

World of Reptiles. REMedia, Inc., 1994.

WORLD WIDE WEB SITES

Destination Florida: Kidstuff. http://www.goflorida.com/kidstuff/

Florida Communities Network. http://fcn.state.fl.us/fcn/

Great Places of Florida: Maps. http://www.grtplaces.com/florida/maps.html

Six Outstanding Florida Kinder-Kind Resorts. http://finefishing.com/fine-trav/northa/usa/florida/florikid/florikid.htm

INDEX

Illustrations, charts, and graphs, are in boldface.

144 ■ FLORIDA